Praise for Invest In The Best

"Fascinating insight into how a professional investor finds great businesses that should stand the test of time. A must-read for anyone with aspirations of becoming a professional investor."

Kyle Caldwell, Deputy Editor, Money Observer

"When I met Keith Ashworth-Lord more than 15 years ago, he really had all of the qualities that a young Warren Buffett had. Patience, discipline and that ability to really look at an investment like he was going to buy the whole company. He could and would dig in to the management, financials, you name it.

I had trademarked Buffettology in 1997, knowing it would be a good investing brand. Keith is the only person I ever gave a licence to use the brand and we are glad that we did. Does he stay on the straight and narrow? As difficult as the last few years have been for investors and finding investments, I would say that the fact the Sanford DeLand UK Buffettology Fund has received multiple awards and is among the top 100 funds says it all. Great job, Keith; now just another 50 years!"

Mary Buffett, Co-author, Buffettology; *CEO/Founder,* Buffett Enterprises, Inc.

"I know of no one on either side of the Atlantic who has embodied the investment methodology of Warren Buffett better than Keith Ashworth-Lord. As far as I am concerned he is the Warren Buffett of the UK. And he has written an absolutely wonderful investment book that is seriously worth reading and rereading. I put it right up there with some of the best books on value investing ever written, including Benjamin Graham's *The Intelligent Investor* and my very own *Buffettology*. If you read only one book on investing this year, I highly recommend that it be Keith's book *Invest in the Best* – it's what we here in the States call a real money maker!"

David Clark, Co-author, Buffettology

"A thoughtful, reliable, and pithy adaptation of the value investing tradition Warren Buffett popularized. Ideally suited for the serious investor as well as managers who care about what such investors think."

Lawrence A. Cunningham, Editor, The Essays of Warren Buffett;
Professor, George Washington University

"Using the stock selection skills that he, and others, have developed over many years Keith Ashworth-Lord has built an impressive performance record as a fund manager. In this practical book Keith describes the key factors that a company must possess before qualifying for inclusion in his portfolio and how he establishes the price that he should pay for their shares. Keith's down to earth style and his enthusiasm make this book accessible to all long-term value investors."

Peter Knapton, Formerly Director of Charities, Pooled Pensions & Consultants, M&G Investments

"*Invest In The Best* gives a fascinating insight into a fund that's unashamedly devoted to applying Warren Buffett's philosophy to the UK stock market. It will appeal to investors who want to develop their investment style and strategy."

Moira O'Neill, Editor, Moneywise

"If you want to master the principles of success in any field, find what has worked best in the past, then customise it. In 1998, Keith and I discovered *Buffettology* by Mary Buffett and David Clark. We read it over and over and over. After that, life analysing the intrinsic value of companies and evaluating their worth relative to their stock market price, was never the same again. Keith has since become a Master Exponent of the best investment blueprint there is. His success with the UK Buffettology Fund proves it conclusively. *Invest in the Best* is the workshop manual behind one of Britain's best-performing funds. Together, they are all you will ever need to become a success yourself in the field of investment."

Jeremy Utton, Founder, Analyst; *Founder and CEO, Prospero*

"Keith Ashworth-Lord's *Invest in the Best* is a superb description of his take on Warren Buffett and Charles Munger's methods for finding the enduring characteristics of a successful business. Among those methods are the strengths and competitive advantages of the business, the business' cash generation potential, and the certainty of future earnings – even before consideration of value and price."

Andrew Kilpatrick, Author, Of Permanent Value: The Story of Warren Buffett

Invest In The Best

Keith Ashworth-Lord graduated with a BSc (Hons) degree in Astrophysics before studying for a Master's degree in Management Studies at Imperial College. His career spans over 30 years in equity capital markets, working in company investment analysis, corporate finance and fund management. He has been Head of Research at Henry Cooke Lumsden and Daiwa Securities and for many years was Chief Analyst at the investment publication *Analyst*. He is a Chartered Fellow of the Chartered Institute for Securities & Investment, having formerly been an individual member of the Stock Exchange. He holds the Investment Management Certificate of the United Kingdom Society of Investment Professionals.

Prior to setting up Sanford DeLand Asset Management Ltd and the UK Buffettology Fund, he was a self-employed consultant working with a variety of stockbroking, fund management and private investor clients. In recent years, he has won four stock picking awards conferred by Thomson-Reuters StarMine. He is regarded as one of the foremost authorities on the investment philosophy of Warren Buffett and Charlie Munger and a keen student of the teachings of Benjamin Graham and Philip Fisher.

Since its launch in March 2011, the UK Buffettology Fund has been a consistent top decile performer in the IA UK All Companies sector and returned 104.85% to 31 December 2015. It was the top performing fund out of 270 in this sector in 2015 and was named 'Best smaller UK Growth Fund 2015' by *Money Observer*. It has been included in the *Investors Chronicle* Top 100 Funds listings for 2014 and 2015.

Keith Ashworth-Lord

Invest In The Best

Applying the principles of Warren Buffett
for long-term investing success

HARRIMAN HOUSE

HARRIMAN HOUSE LTD

18 College Street

Petersfield

Hampshire

GU31 4AD

GREAT BRITAIN

Tel: +44 (0)1730 233870

Email: enquiries@harriman-house.com

Website: www.harriman-house.com

First published in Great Britain in 2016

Copyright © Keith Ashworth-Lord

The right of Keith Ashworth-Lord to be identified as the author has been
asserted in accordance with the Copyright, Design and Patents Act 1988.

Print ISBN: 978-0-85719-484-8

eBook ISBN: 978-0-85719-485-5

British Library Cataloguing in Publication Data

A CIP catalogue record for this book can be obtained from the British Library.

To my son Richard and daughter Anneliese
The best investment I could have made in the future

Every owner of a physical copy of this version of

Invest In The Best

can download the eBook for free direct from us at Harriman House, in a format that can be read on any eReader, tablet or smartphone.

Simply head to:

ebooks.harriman-house.com/investinthebest

to get your free eBook now.

CONTENTS

PREFACE

This book has been written with the aim of guiding the reader through the most important tenets of my investment philosophy. It illustrates the manner in which I set about identifying and selecting companies that I want to own. At the end, you should have a good grasp of the methodology I have synthesised over many years and that, for me, has proven spectacularly successful.

This is not a beginner's guide to investment. It is intended for readers who already have some understanding of the basics, in particular some knowledge of the language of business; namely, accounting. On the one hand, it will be especially helpful to those who have started or managed a business or those who are looking to expand one by reinvestment or acquisition. I am constantly surprised by the number of experienced managers who fail to appreciate the factors that drive value creation. On the other hand, it will aid the conscientious investor who is looking to put together a portfolio of outstanding businesses by showing them the characteristics that crop up repeatedly in the best of businesses. Again, I am constantly surprised by the number of investors who fail to have an anchor line guiding their investment process.

The book starts by describing some seminal events in my past that have had a lasting effect on my way of thinking in the present. It goes on to share the investment epiphany that I experienced when first discovering the Business Perspective Investing system of Benjamin Graham, as practiced by his Berkshire Hathaway disciples Warren Buffett and Charlie Munger.

The main part of the book covers the essentials of what together constitute a superior investment. These include *inter alia* growth, profitability, returns on capital and equity, and cash flow. This part concludes with a look at some of the key financial ratios, the analysis of which tells you how well the company is managing its sales, earnings, assets and cash. A discussion follows about the desirability of a business being predictable to a higher than normal degree of certainty.

The book then moves on from considering the quality of a business to how an enterprise might be valued. Only when this is done is an investor able to compare what might be received in value against what has to be paid in price. Indeed, it might be said that knowing how to value a business is the single most important discipline in investment.

Having identified an excellent business offered at an excellent price, the book concludes with some ideas on how a portfolio might be constructed and why it might need to be changed over time.

INTRODUCTION

I WROTE THIS BOOK ON THE LANAI OVERLOOKING THE swimming pool at my home in Florida. I mention this because had it not been for the success of my investments, I would never have had the wherewithal to purchase a second home in such a wonderful place. Therein lies one of the facts about investment; it is nothing more than deferred consumption. Investing is the art of laying out money today to get a whole lot more back in the future.

To be a successful investor requires very few things. Foremost among them are discipline and patience. For me, discipline comes from investing only from the perspective of a businessman. Patience, however, is the not-so-slight matter of how you are wired.

I bought my first shares at the age of 21 in one of the partial privatisation offerings of BP. At the time I was reading for a Bachelor's degree in Astrophysics, but with that first investment, I was hooked. It was not therefore surprising that a few years later, after a false career start, I emerged with a Master's degree in Management from Imperial College, London. I then chose to make my way in the world of financial services, having become more interested in coupling finance and economics to my mathematical knowledge, rather than physics.

I started out as a trainee investment analyst covering the engineering sector (yes, there was one in those days). As a trainee in the 1980s, you were left to get on with it. Learning on the job was preferred to a structured training scheme. From that humble beginning, I climbed the ladder to Head of Research before broadening out into other industries and trying my hand at corporate finance. It took a little while to realise it but I was flying without a licence. I knew I had to get more professional and set about it by reading the investment ideas of others. In Chapter One, I will add a little more colour to this random walk down Throgmorton Street.

During the years that followed, my investment methodology was cast. Success was due in no small part to having a business partner (Jeremy Utton) who was also profoundly dissatisfied with his investment *modus operandi* at the time. It is no idle boast to say that during this time, we came to be regarded as the foremost exponents of Warren Buffett's investment methodology in the UK.

Having then spent some time consulting in a variety of disciplines – research, asset management and corporate finance – I decided five years ago to set up a new business. Sanford DeLand Asset Management Ltd is named after two proximate townships in Central Florida. It was founded with the aim of launching a fund unashamedly devoted to applying Buffett's philosophy in the UK market. In the four-and-three-quarter years since its inception, the ConBrio Sanford DeLand UK Buffettology Fund has been a consistent top quartile performer. This performance is summarised in the following table.

	UK Buffettology Fund	FTSE All-Share	Relative performance
2011 (9 months)	-12.6%	-6.9%	-6.2%
2012	+34.2%	+8.2%	+22.1%
2013	+36.0%	+16.7%	+21.6%
2014	+1.5%	-2.1%	+3.9%
2015	+28.8%	-2.5%	+41.1%
Overall 2011-15	+104.9%	+12.3%	+82.5%

You don't have to be a rocket scientist to see why the performance has been so good. The reason is simple; I execute a robust investment methodology that concentrates wholly on buying superior businesses at prices that make business sense. My investment credo is that an excellent business bought at an excellent price invariably makes an excellent investment over time.

As Buffett once said:

> "Stocks are simple. All you do is buy shares in a great business for less than the business is intrinsically worth, with managers of the highest integrity and ability. Then you own those shares forever."

I hope that by reading this book, you will be convinced of the logic of concentrating your investments in the very best businesses around, then holding them for the long term.

CHAPTER ONE.

Towards An Investment Philosophy

"If I have seen further than others, it is by standing on the shoulders of giants."

– SIR ISAAC NEWTON

THE EXPERIENCES OF A LIFETIME – SOME FAVOURABLE, SOME unfavourable – exert a profound and lasting influence on what you think about investment. If you began investing near the top of the dot-com boom or shortly before the crash of 1987, you will tend to think that another disaster is always just around the corner. You have been conditioned to be a natural pessimist.

Conversely, if you got rich trading technology stocks in the dot-com boom and managed to avoid the bust, you are more likely to be a natural optimist. The same goes for people like me who got involved in investing and stuck it out through the long secular bull market of 1982-2000. To set the scene, what follows are some of my conditioning life experiences.

A rolling stone gathers no moss

I was born in 1956 into an unremarkable working class family. I watched my parents strive to better their lot and give me the best possible start in life. My grandfather had worked at Bright's cotton mill in Rochdale. He and my grandmother lived in a small rented property owned by the mill. My father saved to help him purchase it outright and upon my grandfather's death in 1964 we inherited the house.

Over the next six years we upped sticks four times, each time endeavouring to 'trade-up'. The disruption and the cost of the whole exercise was painful and pretty obvious to me even at such a tender age. I craved stability.

In 1970, my parents sold their latest house and invested the proceeds in a corner shop selling groceries. The property was rented. The timing could not have been worse. The great inflation was about to start, taking house prices through the roof. And here were mum and dad having exchanged their property-related wealth for ownership of a business that Tesco was about to destroy single handed. Four years later, the shop had to close and the equity was worthless. In their mid to late fifties, they had to start over. In truth, they never recovered.

For me that was a salutary lesson. It is no coincidence that my family has lived in the same home for the last 30 years. Equally it will not surprise you when I say that I believe my parents' traumatic experience is the reason why I am so comfortable with a buy-and-hold investment strategy.

Carpe diem

I was lucky to be born with a gift for learning. I excelled at school in academic subjects and sport. Better still, I was bright enough to realise that therein lay my opportunity for betterment. Having seized my life chance, I graduated from university in 1978, into the teeth of an economic recession and with the Winter of Discontent just around the corner.

Getting a job was tough: one offer out of 130 applications. It was from the newly-nationalised British Aerospace, designing control systems for anti-tank missiles. Though my kids think this is cool, I hated it. Within nine months I was looking for an out. I read an advertisement for an MSc course in Management Science at Imperial College, London. Again, I seized the day: I applied, sat the exam and was offered a place. Imperial was my damascene moment; I discovered economics, accounting and finance. Where had they been all these years?

Getting the Master's degree was one of the easiest things I have ever done. After Imperial, job offers flowed. I was about to train up as an accountant with a US chemicals company. But, at the last minute, I saw an advertisement in the *Financial Times* for an Engineering Investment Analyst with a firm of stockbrokers, Henry Cooke Lumsden, based in Manchester. Curious, I applied and secured an interview.

With all the confidence of someone with a job already in the bag, I learned all about stockbroking and the role of corporate financiers, salesmen, analysts and dealers. More to the point, I saw this was a genuine meritocracy; cut the mustard and you would reap the rewards. Once more, seize the day I thought. I took the job on a much lower starting salary than was being offered by the Americans and I have never regretted doing so.

There is a lesson for investment here as well. Life is a random walk and opportunities crop up in the most unexpected ways at the most unexpected times. When you see one, act. The window of opportunity will not necessarily be open for long.

Equity ownership is a powerful incentive

In the early 1980s, stockbroking firms were partnerships. The partners owned the business and had unlimited liability for its debts. This imparted a sense of responsibility that was wonderful to behold. They kept costs under strict control and would limit their drawings to what the business could support in a normal down year. In an abnormal down year, they would take reduced drawings. In a good year, they would make it up in bonuses.

Big Bang in 1986 was to change all that. Out went unlimited liability; in came outside cash and incorporation. Regrettably the era of the 'professional manager' also dawned. The shots ceased to be called by the Senior Partner as the top job was handed over to a Chief Executive. This resulted in a big hike in salaries, cost-led expansion and empire building. Now a director of the stockbroking side, I watched with horror as our established business – known as 'the Cazenove of the North' – was hitched up to a boutique bank that had only been in existence for a couple of years. Half the equity of the combined group was given away for fool's gold.

With all the inevitability of a Greek tragedy, the recession of the early 1990s revealed just how weak the loan book had been. Thankfully, I could read the accounts and see what was coming. I got my money out just in time. The bank duly went into administration and the stockbroking business was on the way to losing its independence. I had seen a franchise that took 125 years to build brought down in less than 125 weeks. So much for 'professional management'. I know exactly how Arnold Weinstock must have felt when the guys who wrecked Marconi got their hands on the tiller.

I learned that when investing in a business, it is a good idea to check out the equity ownership of the people running it and how much they are drawing in salaries. If they have a large amount of personal wealth tied up in the business and behave frugally, it is more likely that they will act like owners to preserve their wealth (and yours with it).

The rocky road to ruin

Long before the banking debacle, I had learned to be very wary of acquisition-led growth and the opportunities it provides for accounting smoke and mirrors. The 1980s was the era of the mini-conglomerate. An entire genre of businesses sprung up seeking to imitate the success that Hanson Trust and BTR had achieved by bulking up with acquisitions. Names like Williams Holdings, Evered, Tomkins and Suter spring to mind, followed later on by Parkfield, BM Group, Spring Ram, Polly Peck, Coloroll and Thomas Robinson. A handful managed to survive; most didn't.

In those days, I fancied myself as a bit of a rainmaker. Together with two fellow directors of Henry Cooke, we assiduously courted the team that had moved into Thomas Robinson & Son in late 1985, led by Sir Nigel Rudd's brother, Graham. Robinson was an ancient, sleepy engineering business based in my home town. The intention was to use it as the quoted vehicle to build a mini-conglomerate. The deals came thick and fast, and our firm profited handsomely from the fees. Likewise, the profits shot up, fuelled by the acquisitions: £411,000 in 1985; £7.1m in 1986; £12.3m in 1987; £18.0m in 1988; and £25.1m in 1989.

The larger deals were always done with paper, with cash alternatives fully underwritten. What began to worry me was the insatiable appetite of the business for fresh capital. Robinson became a serial rights issuer, returning to the market again and again for additional funds. Despite the marvellous profit record, no cash ever seemed to come out.

Gradually the reason became clear. It wasn't just the machinery that was being manufactured. Robinson was using fair value adjustments to write down acquired stocks and debtors, thus booking greater profits when the stock was sold or the receivables collected. Similarly, by writing down fixed assets, the depreciation charge taken against profits was reduced. In an instant I had learned the distinction between profits and cash.

From 1990 onwards, Robinson faltered with repeated profits warnings and a wholesale change of management. The component businesses were eventually scattered to the four winds as the group was broken up piecemeal. The lesson learned stood me in good stead to later predict the demise of Finelist (which I discuss in Chapter Six) and Independent Insurance. I am happy to say that I have never had an investment go bust underneath me throughout my entire career.

Acquisitions provide a wonderful opportunity for creative accounting and investors should view them warily. Some make great business sense; many don't. As long as you remember Cash is King, you won't go far wrong. No business generating plenty of cash goes under, which cannot be said for businesses generating plenty of profit. Another lesson is that if you are going to invest in a business, you must master the language of business, i.e. accounting.

Beware new paradigms

History is littered with examples of irrational exuberance: 1630s – Tulipomania, 1720s – The South Sea Bubble, 1920s – The Ponzi Scheme, 1960s – Go-Go and 1980s – biotech mania.

The most memorable experience I have lived through is the 1990s dot-com phenomenon. As with most manias, there was a seminal event associated – in this case the coming of the internet and convergence of information and communications technology. The momentum built up by these manias is very powerful and, for many, hard to resist. The dot-com boom-and-bust has to be the single most potent example of 'the greater fool theory' that I have ever witnessed.

You just know something is wrong when investment bankers start devising new ways to value enterprises other than by their ability to generate cash for their owners. Nearly always, the new valuation metric travels further up the income statement and sometimes clean off it.

So you move from earnings after tax, to operating profit, to EBITDA to revenue multiples and worse. At the time, I must have looked like an investment dinosaur. Fortunately, I eschewed the advice of the young men in a hurry and trusted my own abilities. As Ben Graham said, "You are neither right nor wrong because the crowd disagrees with you. You are right because your data and reasoning are right." Shortly after, the emperor was seen to have no clothes.

I think there are a number of lessons contained in this. Firstly, I agree with Sir John Templeton that 'it's different this time' are the four most dangerous words in the investment lexicon. Secondly, history repeats itself but the manifestation is usually different. Thirdly, ignore siren voices and trust your own judgement. And lastly, often the darkest hour is just before the dawn. In investment terms, this means the point where nearly everyone is pessimistic and can see no positive news whatsoever. As the last bull turns to bear, the market inevitably turns up.

Putting lessons into practice

The methodology that I use today has been synthesised from a lifetime of investment experiences. In the mid-1990s, I had been working for over 15 years in investment analysis, had built up a decent personal portfolio as a result of being overpaid in the City and had done so without having the anchor line of a robust investment philosophy.

But how do you go about finding an objective way of identifying investments that can predictably build long-term wealth? I instinctively knew that concentrating on market activity and betting on price action wouldn't do. Also I unequivocally accepted that real investment had to be about taking a part ownership interest in a real business. So, the system had to be one driven first and foremost by the companies themselves and only then by the stock market rewarding astute investment.

The starting point is to identify particular types of company as investment candidates, i.e. those with the most predictable business models, then to value them. If a business model is not predictable to a high degree of certainty, how can you value it? And if you can't value it, how do you know if the stock market price is offering you an investment proposition or not?

On the journey, I read more books on investment than I care to remember. Many weren't worth the candle though occasionally I did pick up something worthwhile to add to the mix.

At that point, fate brought together two like-minded individuals each casting around for a robust investment methodology. The other individual was Jeremy Utton who had founded the subscription investment research publication *Analyst* and now found himself in much the same boat as me. We both had become avid readers and observers of other people's styles, without becoming ardent imitators. We had separately alighted on the teachings of Warren Buffett and Charlie Munger and now set about learning together with the zeal of converts. We worked together on *Analyst* and other projects for the next 11 years. In the process, *Analyst* became synonymous with Warren Buffett in the UK.

Buffettology, the book written by Mary Buffett and David Clark, helped to unlock the mystery. It is an accessible and very simple exposition of Buffett's methodology. It showed us the overriding importance of concentrating on the economics of a business and discarding those companies that do not stack up against a set of predetermined criteria. This was a massive step change in our thinking:

- Away from cheap shares to outstanding companies.

- Away from earnings per share growth rates to cash returns on invested capital.

- Away from allowing random market price movements to determine our actions to letting the underlying business tell us how to act through its operating results.

In a short space of time, I changed from being a securities (or investment) analyst to a business analyst practicing Business Perspective Investing. It was this discipline that kept me away from the dot-com boom-and-bust with its permanent erosion of huge amounts of capital.

Jerry and I made our first journey to the Berkshire Hathaway AGM in 1998, where we had the privilege of meeting Buffett and Munger on home turf. We also developed friendships with a group of individuals collectively known as the Buffettologists in the US because of their devotion to his credo. Then we put on a seminar at London's QE2 Conference Centre in January 1999 entitled 'The Odyssey, the System & the Success of the Buffett-Munger-Graham Investment Phenomenon'. The speakers were six respected Buffettologists: Mary Buffett & Dave Clark, Andy Kilpatrick, Roger Lowenstein, Janet Lowe and Larry Cunningham.

Out of the first of those associations came the launch of the UK Buffettology Fund in March 2011, which I manage true to the principles of Business Perspective Investing. In what follows, I will share with you some of the tenets of Business Perspective Investing, as practiced, and the secrets of its success.

CHAPTER TWO.
Business Perspective Investing

"Investment is most intelligent when it is most business-like."

— Ben Graham, *The Intelligent Investor*

TOO FEW INVESTORS, ANALYSTS OR COMMENTATORS MAKE the distinction between stock market price and underlying business value. The majority of stock market discussion and action among both private and professional investors revolves around price quotes and short-term price targets.

Yet, what is investment if it is not about taking a view on the economic value of a business and then letting the stock market reward operating performance through an appreciation in the share price? In the long run, there is a one-to-one correspondence between the fortunes of a business and the performance of its share price.

Business Perspective Investing is all about investing for the long-term. And if you look at the success of its more famous practitioners over time – people like Ben Graham, John Maynard Keynes, Warren Buffett, Charlie Munger, Bill Ruane and Walter Schloss – you are forced to the conclusion that here is a system that appears to be doing something very right.

In this chapter, I start with an overview of what investment is really all about. In the course of this, you will start to appreciate the more desirable characteristics of a superior business and this will lay the foundations for what follows in the next six chapters.

Business Perspective Investing principles

The craft of investment is to forecast the yield on an asset over the life, or holding period, of the asset. By a process of thorough analysis, the aim is to secure as much safety as possible for your original capital upon which you hope to earn a satisfactory return. It follows that investment is a business venture, not a gamble. It is going to be the enterprises owned that make money for the investor, not the stock market.

The process of determining economic value and then relating it to price is at the heart of Business Perspective Investing. There are a relatively small number of truly outstanding companies and more often than not, their shares can't be bought at attractive prices. Business Perspective Investors know that only an excellent business bought at an excellent price makes an excellent investment in the long run. One without the other just won't do.

We start from the premise that there is no philosophical distinction between part ownership (buying shares in a company) and outright ownership (buying the business in its entirety). Those little pieces of paper called share certificates or those electronic entries on the share register are actually deeds of title. Ownership confers a part interest in a real business. Shares should not be confused with gaming chips.

All we are looking for is pieces of businesses that we really want to own and are able to buy at the right price. If on first inspection we don't like or don't understand what we see, we maintain the discipline to close the book and move on. If we do like and understand what we see, it's onto the next stage. This is to make an assessment of the worth of an investment in the business to a part owner.

Then, and only then, do we check out the price that the stock market is asking us to pay. If we appear to be getting considerably more in value than we are being asked to pay in price, we invest. If not, we step back. It is vital to remember that the price you pay determines the return you get. At any one time, I will have a number of businesses on my watch list that have passed the first 'go: no-go' assessment but where I am waiting for an appropriate pricing opportunity.

This two-stage process naturally divides into analysis of the quality of business and price-to-value ratio determination. The lower the price-to-value ratio, the greater the margin of safety in the investment.

Quality of business

There are several important criteria that companies selected for investment consideration must exhibit in abundance. The list below details the characteristics of quality businesses and I will be looking at these themes in more detail throughout the book.

- Easily comprehensible business model.

- Transparent financial statements.

- Enduring franchise with pricing power born of superior competitive advantage.

- Consistent operational performance with relatively predictable earnings.

- High returns on equity capital employed.

- High proportion of accounting earnings converted into free cash flow.

- Strong balance sheet without unduly high financial leverage.

- Management that acts with the owner's eye and is focused on delivering shareholder value.

- Growth more likely to depend on organic initiatives than frenetic acquisition activity.

I start by recognising that there are businesses and industries that I either will, or will not, understand. I draw a circle around those I know and feel comfortable with. Then I eliminate those businesses within the circle that fall down on the basis of poor management or poor economics. I prefer to keep my circle of competence a foot wide and a mile deep. That way I am much better prepared than someone who has a circle much larger but one that is ill defined around the edges. So, for example, you are unlikely to see me going near oil exploration companies, miners, banks or blue-sky pharmaceutical and biotechnology businesses.

I look for a business where I think I can understand the product, the competition and what might possibly go wrong over time. I want to invest in a great business franchise with high castle walls and a piranha-infested moat with a drawbridge over it. This is the superior competitive advantage mentioned in the list above.

My favourite framework for assessing a company's competitive advantage is the five forces analysis championed by Michael E. Porter in his book *Competitive Strategy*. The lesser the presence of these basic competitive forces, the greater the profit potential of the business. The forces are intense in commodity-like businesses and relatively mild in businesses with rare skills or IP protected products. It is a fact of capitalism that competition continually works to drive down returns towards the cost of capital thus eliminating the potential for profit. To have sustainable, superior earnings power, a business has to possess something very special.

The five interacting forces are as follows:

1. **Threat of new entrants**. Fresh entrants bring new capacity, the desire to win market share and additional resources. Current prices can be deflated or incumbents' costs inflated, thus reducing profitability. Resistance to this threat from quality companies comes from having barriers to entry, such as: scale economies; product differentiation; high capital entry requirements; switching costs for customers; accessible distribution channels; and incumbent cost advantages such as proprietary know-how, learning curve experience or privileged access to input factors.

2. **Intensity of rivalry among existing competitors**. The main tactics include price competition, advertising, new product introductions and enhanced customer service. Price competition is the killer, usually leaving everyone worse off in a race to the bottom. Rivalry is likely to be heightened by factors such as slow industry growth, a large number of competitors, fixed costs necessitating high capacity utilisation and high barriers to exit making it more likely that struggling companies can't afford to quit the game. Where these factors are present, they are warning signs.

3. **Pressure from substitute products**. Substitute products must perform essentially the same function as the product displaced. Their threat is to limit potential returns by imposing a ceiling on the prices that incumbent firms can charge. The more attractive the price/performance of substitutes, the lower the ceiling. Superior companies possess superior products that would-be competitors find hard to challenge and displace.

4. **Bargaining power of customers**. Customers compete with suppliers by forcing down prices or bargaining for higher quality or quantity of goods and services. A buyer is powerful if it accounts for relatively large volumes of a seller's sales or

if its purchases constitute a relatively large amount of its own costs. Therefore, favour companies that have a diversified list of customers. Other factors that come into play are differentiation, switching costs for the customer (which you want to be high) or if the buyer itself operates in a low profitability industry (whereupon it will try to pass the pain onto its suppliers).

5. **Bargaining power of suppliers.** Where suppliers can threaten to raise prices or reduce the quality of purchased goods and services, this is a risk. The conditions making suppliers powerful tend to mirror those that make customers powerful. Ideally you want to have a business that can source its supplies from a range of sources and which adds significant value to these inputs.

I try to appraise how a firm treats its customer and suppliers, as well as to understand the nature and quality of its competitive advantage. Porter's five forces and SWOT (strengths, weaknesses, opportunities and threats) analysis combine to make a powerful tool. This points me in the direction of why a company is making superior returns and it flags up the questions I need to ask management.

On the subject of which, I then ask whether I am joining with management I feel comfortable being in business with. I want superior management to be running the business – management that is able, honest, candid and whose interests align with those of the shareholders.

Having said that, if you have big enough barriers around the franchise, you don't need the ultimate management team to run it. Recall Buffett's sage remark that he likes to buy into businesses that a fool can run because someday a fool will. The trade-off between franchise and manager can sometimes be a bit like pitting the admiral in the dinghy against the deckhand in the speedboat. Ideally, you want to look for able seamen in a vessel that isn't going to capsize.

Following that, as mentioned above, the next step is value determination. I try to decide what seems to represent an appropriate entry price for what I have seen up to that point based on my assessment of what I think the business will earn over the next five, ten or more years. I need to work out whether its earnings power in these future years is likely to be good and getting better, or poor and getting worse. This centres on its growth prospects, profitability of sales and capital, and generation of free cash flow. I attempt to evaluate what the future streams of income and cash flow might be. The barriers to entry and management quality have their biggest bearing on how certain and how predictable those projections into the future are going to be.

Chapters Three to Eight will show you in more detail what to look for in the quest to determine the quality of a business. Figure 2.1 shows Investment's Holy Trinity, which is how I like to conceptually view this quest.

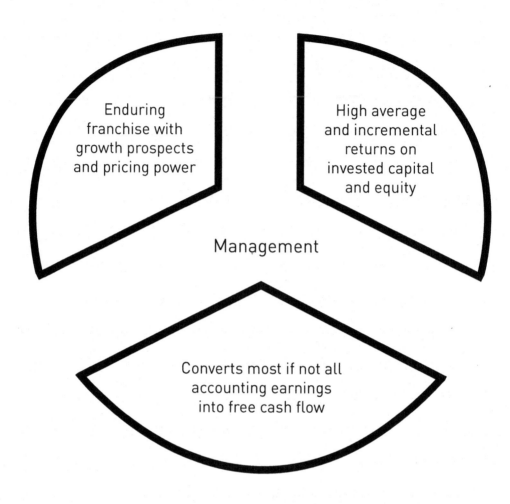

Figure 2.1 – Investment's Holy Trinity

CHAPTER THREE.
Growth Is Not Always What It Seems

"Rapid growth can be a misleading indicator of added value because it can be generated simply by pouring capital into a business."

– G. Bennett Stewart III, *The Quest for Value*

W E HAVE ESTABLISHED THAT GROWTH IS ONE OF THE characteristics we are looking for in a quality business. However, there are caveats to this and care is needed.

Investors have a preoccupation with growth, but few understand its true importance. Indeed, if you were to ask why growth is so important to business valuation, few would be able to give a precise answer.

Investors like companies to be growing because they believe that growth in revenues, profits and earnings is what drives share prices – and nothing else. If a business is expanding most observers believe it is also creating value, but this is not necessarily so. As we shall see in this chapter, companies can grow yet still destroy owner value. Focusing on growth alone neglects the equally important concepts of profitability of capital and free cash flow.

The trade off between growth and profitability

Management's primary objective must be to maximise value creation. The creation of value in a business is the product of growth in earnings multiplied by profitability (defined as the return on capital), less the cost of that capital. How these factors interact is shown in Table 3.1, where the formula used to show this is:

change in value = units of capital × growth rate × (return on capital − cost of capital)

		\multicolumn{9}{c}{Profitability (return on capital)}
		0.0%	2.5%	5.0%	7.5%	10.0%	12.5%	15.0%	17.5%	20.0%
	0.0%	-10.00	-7.50	-5.00	-2.50	0.00	2.50	5.00	7.50	10.00
	2.5%	-10.25	-7.69	-5.13	-2.56	0.00	2.56	5.13	7.69	10.25
G r o w t h	5.0%	-10.50	-7.88	-5.25	-2.63	0.00	2.63	5.25	7.88	10.50
	7.5%	-10.75	-8.06	-5.38	-2.69	0.00	2.69	5.38	8.06	10.75
	10.0%	-11.00	-8.25	-5.50	-2.75	0.00	2.75	5.50	8.25	11.00
r a t e	12.5%	-11.25	-8.44	-5.63	-2.81	0.00	2.81	5.63	8.44	11.25
	15.0%	-11.50	-8.63	-5.75	-2.88	0.00	2.88	5.75	8.63	11.50
	17.5%	-11.75	-8.81	-5.88	-2.94	0.00	2.94	5.88	8.81	11.75
	20.0%	-12.00	-9.00	-6.00	-3.00	0.00	3.00	6.00	9.00	12.00

Note: 100 units of capital employed where the cost of capital is assumed as being 10%.

Table 3.1 – Value created or destroyed at given rates of growth and profitability

The table shows that until the return on capital equals its cost (i.e. all the vertical columns to the left of 10%), growth actually destroys value. Indeed the higher the rate of growth, the more value is destroyed. When the return on capital equals its cost, no value is created or destroyed by growth, which is obvious if you think about it. Beyond the hurdle rate of a 10% return, value is increasingly created with higher rates of growth and profitability.

The other interesting feature of this table is more incremental value is created for a given increase in profitability rather than in the growth rate. Every 2.5% increase in profitability (travelling horizontally across the columns) delivers more in added value than every 2.5% increase in growth (travelling vertically).

If management is overly focused on expanding the boundaries of its empire, i.e. growth, and if that growth is taking place at returns on capital beneath its cost, value is being destroyed. This value destruction will be reflected in the price of the equity capital (i.e. the share price), which will be devalued by the stock market to the point where the capital sells at the going rate of return available elsewhere in the economy. A growing company whose share price consistently sells at beneath its net asset value is almost certainly reinvesting capital for unacceptable returns. Investors are better off putting their capital to work elsewhere.

Alternatively, if management is overly focused on getting an immediate return from its investment in new projects, i.e. profitability, it risks eschewing projects that need time for their returns to build up to an acceptable level and beyond. In this instance, it will forgo long-term growth in pursuit of short-term gratification. It will likewise forgo the opportunity of taking market share, leaving itself open to competitive threat in the future.

Where companies cannot always have more growth and higher returns simultaneously, good management judgement about the returns that will flow from the investments made is crucial. From the investor's point of view, good judgement of management quality in this respect is vital to the success of the investment decision.

Earnings are not created equal

The traditional accounting model of company valuation says that share prices are determined by capitalising accounting earnings at an appropriate price-to-earnings ratio (PER). Growth of earnings thus becomes the Holy Grail for traditional investors. For example, the GARP school of investment managers looks for stocks that offer 'growth at a reasonable price'. Note there is no mention of returns on invested capital.

But as we have seen, earnings taken in isolation from the profitability of capital are a misleading indicator of performance. Although companies that sell for the highest price-to-earnings ratio (PER) multiples are often growing rapidly, rapid growth by itself is not enough to guarantee a high multiple.

Take two hypothetical businesses Sanford and DeLand. Both currently have the same earnings and are expected to report the same earnings growth rate. Should they be valued on the same PER multiple? The accounting model of valuation would say so. But suppose that Sanford has to invest twice as much capital as DeLand to achieve that growth rate. Or put another way, for the same amount of capital invested, DeLand generates twice the rate of growth as Sanford. Should DeLand command twice the PER multiple of Sanford?

Sanford is spending its way to the growth that DeLand manages to achieve by more efficient use of capital. One glance at Table 3.2 shows that the cash performance (for simplicity measured as earnings less necessary new capital investment) of DeLand leaves Sanford standing over time. It is clearly the more valuable business but a focus on earnings and their growth rate alone does not capture this. (Fortunately there is another methodology that does – the economic model of company valuation – and we will meet this in Chapter Four.)

	Year	1	2	3	4	5
Sanford	Earnings	10.0	11.0	12.1	13.3	14.6
	Re-investment	5.0	5.5	6.1	6.6	7.3
	Cash flow	5.0	5.5	6.0	6.7	7.3
DeLand	Earnings	10.0	11.0	12.1	13.3	14.6
	Re-investment	2.5	2.7	3.0	3.3	3.7
	Cash flow	7.5	8.3	9.1	10.0	10.9

Table 3.2 – Earnings and cash performance of Sanford and DeLand (£m)

A capital intensive company, such as Sanford, may need to use much of its cash flow to reinvest in productive assets to maintain its earnings power. Conversely, a company with a different shape, like DeLand, may have very little fixed asset needs, so that its cash flow becomes available for acquisitions or returning to shareholders as dividends or buybacks.

Cash flow only really becomes valuable once it becomes distributable. Business owners cannot spend factories, stock or debtors. This means the growth that is produced by businesses that simply grow their assets other than cash, yet stand still in value, is worthless to investors.

You can see where this is leading. Managers of companies with slower intrinsic growth can boost their apparent returns by throwing more capital at the business. Hence the relevance of that opening quotation from Bennett Stewart.

At the personal level, you can think of it like this. Suppose you wish to grow your income by £10 next year and you have £400 of spare cash left over from last year's endeavours. You can obtain that £10 of growth by investing £200 in a 5% savings account and then go out and enjoy spending the other £200. Alternatively, you can deposit £400 in a 2.5% savings account and still produce the extra tenner at the year-end. Which makes the greater business sense? It is obvious: invest at higher returns and pay yourself a dividend.

This throwing of more capital at the business is often done by acquisitions, which make less than ideal business sense. Worse still, if that capital is earning less than its opportunity cost, any growth produced actually destroys owner value, as we saw in Table 3.1. You can think of opportunity cost as the rival savings account offering a higher rate of interest.

Growth for its own sake: example of Rentokil Initial plc

City analysts concentrate far too heavily on earnings growth rather than cash performance when undertaking valuations and making investment recommendations. But managers are as much to blame for taking all this in. Many managers get hooked on making acquisitions to try to accelerate the growth rates of their companies, which distracts them from the principles that made their businesses successful in the first place, i.e. selling profitable products that satisfy customers' needs from a tight capital base.

The experience of Rentokil Initial in the mid-1990s is illustrative of this. Rentokil acquired BET (a business twice its size) in the middle of 1996. Prior to that, Clive

Thompson (Rentokil's CEO) had earned himself the sobriquet 'Mr. 20%'. This had been Rentokil's annual earnings growth rate over the previous 14 years, an achievement that had made it one of the UK's most admired companies.

But BET was an acquisition too far. Although the enlarged group's overall earnings per share continued to rise by around 20% immediately after acquisition, the price in terms of dilution for Rentokil shareholders was massive. Profitability and cash flow were decimated. This is shown in Table 3.3.

Year to December	1994	1995	1996	1997	1998
Sales	735	875	2,340	2,875	2,899
Operating profit	176	210	342	449	504
Operating margin (%)	24.0	24.0	14.6	15.6	17.4
Pre-tax profit	177	215	318	417	491
Earnings	115	139	219	295	350
Earnings margin (%)	15.6	15.9	9.4	10.2	12.1
Earnings per share (p)	5.9	7.1	8.6	10.3	12.2
Growth (%)	+20.8	+21.1	+20.5	+20.4	+18.4
Cash earnings	87	117	122	234	232
Average equity	390	491	1,438	2,413	2,664
Sales per £1 of equity (p)	188.2	178.3	162.7	119.1	108.8
Earnings per £1 of equity (p)	29.4	28.4	15.2	12.2	13.1
Cash earnings per £1 of equity (p)	22.3	23.9	8.5	9.7	8.7

Table 3.3 – Rentokil Initial plc financial performance, 1994-1998 (£m unless stated)

Return on average equity, shown here as earnings per £1 of equity, fell sharply from 28.4% in 1995 to 15.2% in 1996 and to 12.2% in 1997. Cash earnings per £1 of average equity fell even more sharply from 23.9p in 1995 to 8.5p in 1996 and 9.7p in 1997. The 'economic value-added' produced in the year of acquisition, and indeed since, from combining the businesses has not just been zero, it has been negative.

Accounting earnings growth continued for a time simply because a large amount of cheap, tax-efficient debt was used to pay for the acquisition. Although the returns were above the cost of debt, the incoming business generated no retainable cash, so the original, highly profitable Rentokil businesses were forced to divert their surplus cash flows to servicing and repaying the BET debt instead of being made available to owners. This growth at any cost proved a disaster for investors.

To this day, Rentokil Initial has not recovered to produce sustained growth. Revenues have been range-bound at £1.7bn to £2.5bn ever since the acquisition as various management teams have tried to rationalise the portfolio. Likewise, earnings per share have never risen back above the 16.5p recorded in 2003 and dividends have been erratic.

This is captured by the share price performance in Figure 3.1. The chart also shows that despite the warning signs being there in 1996 and 1997, it took a further couple of years to start being reflected in the share price. This is a common theme in investing: you can see something is going to happen but you don't know quite when.

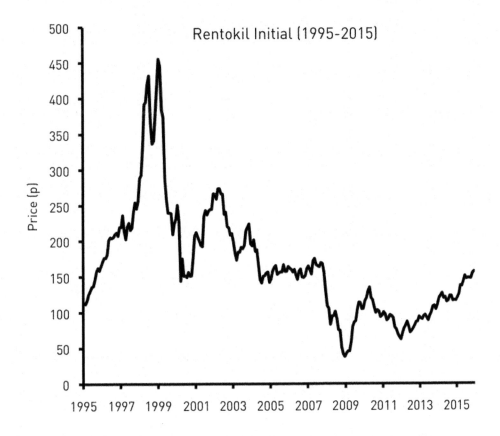

Figure 3.1 – Rentokil Initial share price, 1995-2015 (monthly average)

Growth and profitability drive value creation

A company that grows its revenues, earnings and capital base rapidly will be worth more than a slow growing company as long as they are both earning the same rate of return on invested capital and as long as this rate of return is materially higher than the opportunity cost of capital.

Growth will add to the economic value of a business if the returns on incremental investment continue to be comfortably in excess of the investor's opportunity cost of capital. In other words, as long as the company's retained earnings are better off being invested back into the business rather than being paid out to shareholders and then reinvested elsewhere. Moreover, such reinvestment elsewhere will have attracted tax when paid out as dividends whereas retained earnings reinvested into the business will not.

Some businesses are very good at creating value; others are not. As we have seen with the Sanford and DeLand example earlier, the earnings growth rates of two companies can in theory be identical (or in reality very similar), yet their market values might differ enormously. The difference lies in the rates of return on capital invested and the amount of cash generated for each unit of capital invested. Operating margins could be declining in one business, expanding in the other. The ratio of sales to assets could be expanding in one business, declining in the other. If the two were retailers, the key difference might be in stock turnover, debtor days or asset utilisation.

Given equal growth rates in revenues, companies that earn a higher return on their capital relative to their cost of capital should command higher stock market values. It follows then that both growth and profitability should drive economic, and therefore stock market, value.

Some businesses don't grow at all, because they operate in mature markets, earn huge spreads on their capital, have little need to invest and spew out cash. Just because they are not growing it does not mean that they have little value. On the contrary, these businesses are like annuities: they may not show much growth but they still deliver a little changed level of cash income, year in, year out.

Some companies forgo growth opportunities because they prefer to generate cash in the short-term. But had they invested in those opportunities, their depressed short-term cash flows may well have developed into much longer-term cash flows. Sometimes it can be worth investors accepting less jam today for much more jam tomorrow.

To reiterate, businesses that grow, earn low rates of return on their asset base and produce little or no free cash are intrinsically close to worthless as investments.

Businesses that are stable and which earn a modest spread over and above their opportunity cost of capital are likely to have modest values. Businesses that grow, have high returns on their capital and produce an abundance of free cash are highly valuable.

The fundamentals of growth

All growth starts with sales or revenues. Sales produce profits, earnings and cash flows. Without sales, none of these other value enhancing variables can be created.

To generate sales, a business must offer a product or service that has compelling appeal to its chosen customers at prices that deliver utility to those customers and make economic sense for the provider company. Growth can easily be generated by selling products at very low prices that make no economic sense at all for the supplier. Utility has to be delivered to customers in a way that bypasses competitive products or services too, otherwise destructive price competition establishes itself pretty quickly.

On the supply side, these are the main ways for a company to achieve organic sales growth:

1. **Produce and sell more units of the same product or service**. This is the least risky form of sales growth. A company will already have established market acceptability for its products. The incremental cost of producing the next unit is usually restricted to its variable costs, so margins on these incremental sales can be very attractive. The main commercial risks are if the business has to go into new markets, e.g. overseas.

2. **Sell the same products and services at higher prices**. There may be resistance by existing customers to higher prices. If the business delivers 'must-have' products to its customers and that same level of utility is not provided by competitive offerings, then price increases are likely to stick well.

3. **Sell to new customers who have not bought in the past**. The company may be able to find new target markets for its products that allow it to sell higher volumes and at higher prices: this is a double-whammy. Differential pricing is not easy to achieve, though. To be successful, there must not be transparency between separate markets.

4. **Develop and sell new products and services**. This is the most risky form of achieving sales growth. New products increase costs, the risk of failure and the risks of establishing new customers and a new competitive advantage.

On the demand side, the main ways to generate growth are:

1. **Be competitive**. The price of the product has to be competitive with other offerings if there are any. It has to be competitive in terms of the utility it delivers and it has to be competitive in terms of all its input costs.

2. **Price the product for its target market**. The product has to dovetail with the wealth and disposable income of the market it is aimed at. If the consumers or the businesses to which the product is being aimed do not have enough discretionary resources to enable them to buy it, then the company is wasting its time – and its owners' capital.

3. **Avoid fads**. The product might pander to current tastes, which can be fickle. Chains of fashion stores, for example, come and go in popularity according to whether they are considered chic. Fashion businesses generally are not good long-term investments because they lack high predictability beyond a few years. Growth in revenues, profits and earnings needs to be consistent over a reasonable period of time in order to be able to value a series of cash coupons going forward.

As ever, it will pay investors to keep their understanding of these key investment issues simple. In that way, they can be used practically. Controlled growth is good, though worthless without being connected to profitability and to cash generation. The package of all three can be expensive for investors if the combined value they create cannot be bought in the stock market for much less than it is worth.

CHAPTER FOUR.
Profitability Of Capital Drives Shareholder Value

"If a firm has a high return on capital and has had for a long time, there is a prima facie case for saying that it is a good business, and is always likely to be a good investment."

– RICHARD KOCH, *SELECTING SHARES THAT PERFORM*

M OST INVESTORS THINK ABOUT PROFITABILITY IN TERMS of how much profit a company earns out of every £1 of revenue it generates. This is indeed a measure of profitability – profitability of sales – but it focuses exclusively on the profit and loss account.

There is another measure of profitability: the return on capital (or the net assets employed in the business). This measures how well the company is managing its balance sheet. It is the interaction of growth and profitability as measured by the return on capital that determines real value creation in a business and this is what we will examine in this chapter.

Capital intensity and free cash flow

Let's return to our hypothetical companies Sanford and DeLand. Given identical growth rates, a business that earns higher profits per £1 of capital invested will be worth more than one that earns lower profits per £1 of invested capital.

Put another way, the less capital you have at risk to generate a given level of sales and earnings, the better off you are because your return for each £1 invested is higher and so the free cash flow generated will be higher too. It is free cash that ultimately determines value.

Table 4.1 demonstrates the interaction between growth and profitability where we consider three companies that are all growing their earnings at 10% per annum. Although the earnings growth rates are identical, the reinvestment requirements of each to support this growth differ.

This time, both Sanford and DeLand start with £50m of invested capital. To produce the growth, the more capital-intensive Sanford must add to its capital base by 10% p.a. whereas 5% p.a. suffices for the less capital-intensive DeLand. All other things being equal, comparing Year 5 with Year 1 shows DeLand has grown its free cash by £4.1m whereas Sanford has only managed £2.3m. This leaves DeLand generating 1.59 times the amount of free cash that is coming from Sanford in Year 5.

In reality, if the reinvestment requirement of DeLand is half that of Sanford, it is unlikely that to get them to the starting blocks at Year 1 the capital base of each will be identical. For DeLand to get to £10m of earnings will have required less capital along the way than Sanford.

This is shown by a third hypothetical company, Castlefield. It starts with £25m of capital, which then grows by 5% p.a. to support its 10% earnings growth. Over the five years, Castlefield grows its free cash by £4.3m to the point where it is generating 1.79 times the amount of cash coming from Sanford in Year 5.

Since dividends and returns of surplus capital are paid out of free cash, not accounting earnings, this shows that Castlefield is becoming progressively more valuable than DeLand, which in turn is becoming progressively more valuable than Sanford. It is also reflected in the quantum and increase of returns on average capital employed.

	Year	1	2	3	4	5
Sanford	Earnings	10.0	11.0	12.1	13.3	14.6
	Capital base before	50.0	55.0	60.5	66.6	73.2
	Re-investment	5.0	5.5	6.1	6.6	7.3
	Capital base after	55.0	60.5	66.6	73.2	80.5
	Cash flow	5.0	5.5	6.0	6.7	7.3
	Return on av. capital (%)	*19.0*	*19.0*	*19.0*	*19.0*	*19.0*
DeLand	Earnings	10.0	11.0	12.1	13.3	14.6
	Capital base before	50.0	52.5	55.1	57.9	60.8
	Re-investment	2.5	2.6	2.8	2.9	3.0
	Capital base after	52.5	55.1	57.9	60.8	63.8
	Cash flow	7.5	8.4	9.3	10.4	11.6
	Return on av. capital (%)	*19.5*	*20.4*	*21.4*	*22.4*	*23.5*
Castlefield	Earnings	10.0	11.0	12.1	13.3	14.6
	Capital base before	25.0	26.2	27.5	28.9	30.4
	Re-investment	1.2	1.3	1.4	1.5	1.5
	Capital base after	26.2	27.5	28.9	30.4	31.9
	Cash flow	8.8	9.7	10.7	11.8	13.1
	Return on av. capital (%)	*39.0*	*40.9*	*42.8*	*44.9*	*47.0*

Table 4.1 – Capital employed, reinvestment requirements and free cash flow (£m unless stated)

Economic goodwill

Companies that generate above average returns on capital are worth considerably more than the book value of their assets. In the main, such companies do not rely on physical plant and machinery to generate the high returns – their USP is much more intangible. They rely on being able to offer something that is unique or proprietary. In short, they possess economic goodwill and this is what enables them to charge premium prices and generate exceptional returns for their shareholders.

If that were not the case, the charging of premium prices for a non-differentiated product or service would attract other entrants. Thereupon excess returns would be competed away to the cost of capital, i.e. driven down to the point where no profit potential existed any longer.

Note that economic goodwill should not be confused with accounting goodwill. At best, accounting goodwill remains static on the balance sheet because it is merely a bookkeeping entry representing the premium paid by the acquirer of a business, where the consideration exceeds the net assets being acquired.

As long as a company's reputation for quality of service remains intact, economic goodwill will increase as the company reaches out to more and more customers.

Franchises possessing large economic goodwill become more valuable over time because they usually combine earning power with a small appetite for additional capital. This is because their USP often relies on intangible qualities that are hard for would-be competitors to replicate. Conversely, businesses that are capital-intensive, as demonstrated by having a high ratio of fixed and working capital to sales, tend to earn lower rates of return on those assets. They require a large amount of additional capital each year just to stay in business.

Great, good and bad uses of capital

Let's consider what differentiates businesses in terms of profitability of capital. Great businesses are those that absorb very little new capital yet consistently produce superb returns. The shape I covet most has a scalable offering, which is tough for rivals to compete with, plus a low level of cost (especially fixed cost).

These franchises rely on intellectual capital like the skill of the employees, must-have products, proprietary technology or owning a piece of their customers' minds. Returns tend to be high and cash generation copious because of the modest reinvestment requirements. They just give back more and more cash each year without requiring you to put up much at all. There is no adverse impact on their business returns from inflation or deflation, nor from the replacement cycle, which hammers so many fixed-asset-heavy businesses. Examples of these great businesses would be Hargreaves Lansdown, RWS Holdings, Bioventix or Games Workshop.

A good business is one that takes capital but where the return it generates on that capital is highly satisfactory and well above the company's cost of capital. These are also perfectly satisfactory from an investment angle. Examples include Rotork, Spirax-Sarco Engineering, Victrex and A.G. Barr.

A bad business is one that is forced to grow just to stay in the game and where management is investing capital at a rate of return that is below the cost of capital and, in the worst cases, below what investors could earn risk-free on the street. They are effectively mortgaging tomorrow's cash flow to prop up yesterday's poor operating performance. So-called smokestack industries, steel or textiles exemplify these economically unattractive enterprises. To have any sort of edge requires that the other input factor – labour – is cheap, hence their migration away from the developed economies.

Profitable growth

As we have seen, growth of earnings is just the product of volume of capital invested times the rate of return achieved on that capital.

Companies can manufacture growth by pumping large amounts of capital into low-return projects. This kind of growth is not worth much because it can only be sustained by throwing more and more capital at projects without an economic rate of return. These projects can involve capital expenditure on more productive assets or acquisitions. This manufactured growth produces growth in earnings, but, as the shareholders in Rentokil discovered, the cash dries up and eventually the stock market cottons on. At that point it devalues the market price of the capital by causing the shares to fall – sometimes to zero!

The most prized growth for the investor is that coming from trusting more capital to an able management that can deploy the capital under its stewardship at very attractive rates of return. Sometimes this can be in the form of a 'land grab' – capturing a large share of the available market before the competition has time to react – or from a progressive roll-out. This then ramps up profitability as economies of scale are garnered.

A good example is Domino's Pizza Group, which has established itself as the No.1 brand in the highly competitive UK takeaway pizza market, ahead of Pizza Hut, Papa John's and Perfect Pizza. The features of the Domino's franchise model that make it so successful and attractive to investors are as follows:

1. Enduring competitive advantage, based on quality of ingredients, response time, reputation and the harnessing of sophisticated ordering technology. You get the same offering whichever store you buy from.

2. Roll-out potential – more than an eight-fold increase in UK store numbers over 20 years. Yet there is still significant growth potential in the UK and Ireland, towards 1,200 stores.

3. Stores' capital investment is borne by the franchisees. The parent company needs capital only for infrastructure.

4. The parent company takes approximately 40% of stores' sales through royalties, franchise fees, sale of ingredients, property leasing and IT systems.

5. There are margin benefits from economies of scale.

6. There is strong cash generation allowing a progressive dividend policy and periodic returns of capital to shareholders.

Table 4.2 shows how these strengths have been reflected in Domino's financial results over the last ten years. The moderation in performance since 2011 is due to having acquired loss-making Master Franchises for Germany and Switzerland, in the process incurring £20.2m of operating losses in four years. This is yet more evidence of the dangers of acquisition-led growth.

Year to December	2005	2006	2007	2008	2009	2010	2011	2012	2013	2014
Growth:										
Average number of stores open	382	429	476	527	581	637	696	766	832	876
Av. weekly unit sales (£'000)	10.7	11.3	12.5	13.5	14.1	15.2	15.6	15.3	16.4	17.7
Turnover	81.7	95.0	114.9	136.0	155.0	188.6	209.9	240.5	266.8	294.4
(Growth %)	+10.0	+16.3	+21.0	+18.4	+14.0	+21.7	+11.3	+14.6	+10.9	+10.3
Operating profit	10.8	14.0	18.7	23.6	29.5	37.8	42.0	46.8	47.3	54.4
(Growth %)	+20.0	+29.3	+33.2	+26.1	+25.1	+28.4	+11.2	+11.3	+1.0	+15.1
Earnings per share (p)	5.1	6.1	8.5	10.9	13.8	17.4	19.5	22.2	26.2	26.1
(Growth %)	+22.5	+19.9	+38.9	+28.2	+27.1	+25.7	+12.2	+13.8	+18.4	-0.4

Year to December	2005	2006	2007	2008	2009	2010	2011	2012	2013	2014
Profitability:										
Operating profit margin (%)	13.3	14.8	16.3	17.3	19.0	20.0	20.0	19.5	17.6	18.5
Return on average equity (%)	61.6	113.0	145.5	155.1	137.7	99.9	78.9	64.9	70.2	60.6
Cash flow:										
Free cash flow generated	9.0	12.6	16.4	7.8	9.9	24.9	18.4	26.5	34.6	58.2
Conversion of accounting earnings to free cash flow (%)	108	127	123	46	46	92	59	74	81	135
Returns to shareholders:										
Net profit after tax & minorities	8.3	9.9	13.4	16.8	21.6	27.1	31.3	36.0	43.0	43.2
Share buy-backs	8.2	10.2	8.4	3.8	7.6	4.7	2.2	3.3	0.0	2.2
Dividends	3.2	4.2	5.8	8.0	10.5	13.6	18.0	21.8	24.6	27.5
Total returned to shareholders	11.4	14.4	14.2	11.8	18.1	18.3	20.2	25.1	24.6	29.7
Return as % of net profit	138	146	106	70	84	68	65	70	57	69

Table 4.2 – Domino's Pizza Group plc, selected financial performance statistics 2005-14 (£m unless stated)

How the stock market has rewarded the financial performance of Domino's is shown in Figure 4.1.

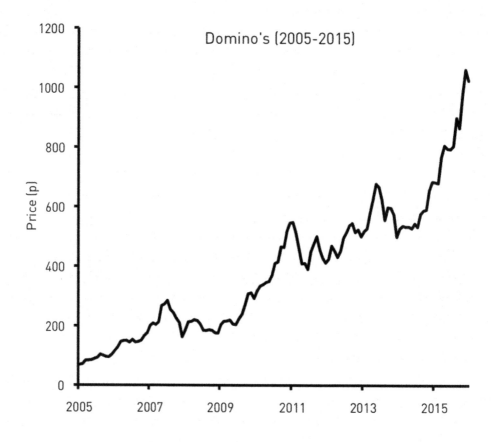

Figure 4.1 – Domino's Pizza Group share price, 2005-2015 (monthly average)

Return on capital: risk and reward

The purpose of new investment must be creation of greater shareholder wealth. Greater wealth will only accrue if and when the returns made on new investment by a company exceed the returns freely available from investing the money elsewhere. This represents the opportunity cost of capital and is a familiar concept in economics and investing.

Enterprises operate in competitive markets. That does not just mean markets for outputs such as goods and services, but also markets for inputs such as raw materials, labour and, crucially, finance. Financial resources flow downhill to projects offering the prospect of the most lucrative returns. Why should an investor settle for poor returns when there is better on offer elsewhere? Of course, some of the potentially superior returns may well entail potentially greater risks – there is a trade-off here.

When you sink your money into a business venture, you inevitably take on risk. Will the monthly sales targets be met? Will the production line keep turning without breaking down? Will the finance director screw up? Will some new product development render this company's product obsolete? Taking on such risks necessitates that you demand adequate rewards.

Some investors are risk averse and cannot stomach the idea of losing some or all of their investment. Generically, these have been dubbed widows and orphans. Buffett agrees with Harry S. Truman on this point; if you can't stand the heat, stay out of the kitchen. Conversely, more gung-ho types may claim to be attracted to risk, using supposedly superior evaluation techniques to arbitrage the ignorance of others and thus secure high compensation. Hedge funds fall into that category.

Business Perspective Investors tread the middle ground, seeking to fence off as much risk as possible whilst still making decent returns. They define risk as business risk, not risk associated with stock market price fluctuations that bear little correlation to the economic realities of the business in question. They believe that ultimately economic value and share prices converge; they just don't know when it will happen. Business Perspective Investors look for above average returns predictable to a high degree of certainty and carrying the lowest possible risk of permanent capital loss.

Components of cost of capital

It is normal that as businesses mature, more capital gets added at incrementally lower rates of return. This continues until the marginal rate of return equals the cost of capital. At this point, sources of new capital start to dry up because rational providers see no prospect of earning super-normal returns and they shift their capital elsewhere.

Starved of capital and without the high returns, earnings growth quickly falls away. Relatively capital-light businesses will still be able to generate free cash for an extended period because they have less need for maintenance capital expenditure. But capital-intensive businesses remain hungry – and the prognosis for them at this point is bleak.

The next question, then, is what is and what determines the cost of capital? Quite simply, it is the minimum return on capital that investors are prepared to accept from the company in question. It is the hurdle that must be cleared before any value starts to be added by the company deploying that capital into projects. The greater the risk that the company invites its investors to bear, the greater the potential reward that it must offer, and vice versa. Ergo, the investor's expected return is the company's cost of capital. There are three essential components that make up the cost of capital:

1. The cost of capital for business risk

2. The cost of debt

3. The cost of equity

The cost of capital for business risk represents compensation for uncertainty. Since all business activity is inherently risky, investors are unable to predict with absolute certainty the future levels of profit after tax and cash flow. The compensation required does not depend upon how the company chooses to finance itself. It can be estimated by adding a business risk premium to the risk-free return available on government bonds.

The cost of debt is compensation for the credit risk that the company might default on its obligations to pay interest and repay principal in a timely manner. To determine the cost of debt is straightforward: it is the post-tax yield to maturity of the company's long-term debt obligations. Interest payments are set against operating profits before being taxed. This tax shelter explains why the cost of debt, unlike the cost of equity, is struck after tax. The coupon (interest rate) that providers of debt offer will depend, inter alia, upon the company's credit score rating as determined by debt agencies such as Moody's, Standard & Poor's and Fitch. For traded debt, e.g. the 'A' and 'B' Loan Notes issued by Dignity plc that we discuss in Chapter Seven, you can look up the yield to maturity on a daily basis.

The cost of equity is compensation for business risk plus a premium for financial risk reflecting the fact that shareholders stand at the bottom of the capital provider hierarchy. From already variable operating profits, the company has to discharge its obligations firstly to HM Revenue & Customs as tax, secondly to lenders as interest and thirdly to non-equity providers of capital, such as minorities and preference shareholders, as dividends. The earnings left for ordinary shareholders come after all these prior claims, making them the most volatile, and hence riskiest, of all. It follows that equity is the most expensive class of capital because of the equity risk premium demanded by ordinary shareholders for shouldering additional risk.

Academics have feasted on devising models to accurately portray the cost of equity. It is central to the Capital Asset Pricing Model (CAP-M), devised by William Sharpe in 1964 and building on the earlier work of Harry Markowitz. With its introduction of sophisticated mathematical formulae and Greek letters, Buffett pithily remarked how the high priests of finance like to cow the laity with their use of symbolism. Buffett considers CAP-M type reasoning to be nonsense, with genuine risk coming from not knowing what you are doing. Others ask why, if the academics are so clever, is Buffett the world's most successful investor and they are still on the public payroll?

Being a humble soul, I take a very simplistic view: a realistic equity investor should be looking for a total annual return of somewhere in the range of 8-10%. So taking 10% as the cost of equity is a reasonable stab. Better to be approximately right like this than precisely wrong from the CAP-M equations.

The blended cost of a company's debt and equity in proportion to the amount of each employed in the capital structure is known as the weighted average cost of capital. It is often used as the rate to discount future streams of cash flow back to net present value.

Substituting debt for equity

No matter how high the cost of debt, the cost of equity will always be higher because of the additional risk being borne. In addition, interest payments provide a valuable tax shelter. That is why it can make sense for companies to gear up to buy back shares. As long as the level of indebtedness is such that the gross interest payments are comfortably covered by operating profit (i.e. the interest cover is sufficient), it will benefit shareholders by leveraging the returns to equity. The example in Table 4.3 shows this.

Company X	No debt	Debt
Operating profit	10.0	10.0
Interest payable	0.0	(1.0)
Profit before tax	10.0	9.0
Tax @ 20%	(2.0)	(1.8)
Profit after tax	8.0	7.2
Weighted shares in issue (m)	100	80
Earnings per share (p)	8.0	9.0

Table 4.3: Capital structure and its impact on earnings (£m unless stated)

Company X has 100m shares in issue. With a share price of 100p, the market capitalisation is £100m. Profit after tax is £8.0m, giving earnings per share (EPS) of 8.0p. The PER is therefore 12.5x. In the first column, X employs no debt in its capital structure but relies entirely on equity financing. In the second column X has borrowed £20m at an interest rate of 5.0% and used the money to buy back 20m of its own shares at 100p each.

The profit after tax has fallen by £800,000. But the number of shares in issue has also gone down to 80m. So EPS has increased from 8.0p to 9.0p. This 12.5% enhancement is entirely due to the fact that the post-tax cost of debt, 5.6%, is cheaper than the pre-tax cost of equity for X in its ungeared state.

The PER might adjust downwards from 12.5x because X will be viewed as a more risky proposition with the lender now ahead of ordinary shareholders in the pecking order. But with interest cover of 10.0 times, the level of debt would be seen as comfortable and any impact on the PER would not be such as to wipe out the EPS enhancement. To eliminate it completely, the PER would have to fall to 11.1x, which is unlikely.

The enterprise value of X, when geared, is the £90m market value of its equity (80m shares x PER of 12.5 x EPS of 9.0p) plus the £20m value of its debt. Originally it was £100m, now it is £110m. So where has the extra £10m of value come from? The answer is from HM Revenue & Customs in the form of a tax credit of £200,000 per annum for the interest expense. As long as the business model is not disturbed and the tax rules don't change, this extra £200,000 will accrue annually in perpetuity. The additional £10m is the present value of that future stream of extra cash.

To take full advantage of debt to maximise shareholder value, companies should borrow if they are able to, not because they have to. In fact, the fewer requirements a company has to raise capital for expansion, the more money it should borrow. As soon as more free cash is generated than can be reinvested for profitable growth, the cash could be used to service more debt with its substantial tax sheltering advantage. The capital can then be used to pay special dividends, or to retire equity thus allowing future earnings to be shared out among fewer owners.

Crucially, though, the strategy only makes sense if equity is being retired at sensible prices. Too many companies pay too little attention to the price they pay when buying back their shares.

Bennett Stewart, senior partner of consultants Stern Stewart & Co, had this to say about the situation: "Neglecting debt's tax benefit is one sure way for a strong surplus cash generator to attract the attention of unwanted suitors."

Return on capital employed (ROCE)

The basic definition of capital employed can be looked at from two angles: assets and obligations. Each is equally valid.

From the assets standpoint:

capital employed = fixed assets + net working capital + cash

From this angle, it represents all the productive assets utilised by the business.

From the obligations standpoint:

capital employed = gross debt + provisions + non-equity capital + equity capital

From this angle, it represents all the capital and debt that have been invested in those assets.

The return is operating profit plus any interest received on cash, the latter effectively being shareholder equity that has been placed on deposit at the bank.

The importance of return on capital employed is that it gauges the return being generated on all assets irrespective of how those assets are being financed. For example, if a company takes on new debt at 5% and invests it for a return of only 8%, it will nonetheless generate more in extra profit than it will pay in extra interest. This will benefit the return to equity by the difference (after tax). But 8% is a poor investment return and the higher gearing has increased the risk borne by the equity shareholders. So are they really that better off? If this operation to gear up at 5% and invest at 8% has diluted the overall returns, this will show up in the ROCE analysis.

To show this, take a company that has 100 units of capital on which it earns a return of 10 units (i.e. a 10% ROCE). Suppose it borrows a further 20 units of capital at 5% upon which it earns a return of 8%. Its earnings will now be increased by the capital borrowed times the spread (8% - 5% = 3%). This increases its earnings from the original 10 units to 10.6 units. But this will have been achieved on 120 units of capital, so the ROCE is 10.6 ÷ 120 = 8.83%.

Return on equity (ROE)

I have come to the conclusion that return on equity is like the rifle to the scattergun that is return on capital employed. Both are important tools of analysis but ROE is so much more specific because it concentrates exclusively on how good, or otherwise, management is at compounding your equity investment. That means working for you, the ordinary shareholder, not the bank manager, the preference shareholder, the loan stock holder or the minority interest. The superior company will earn a superior return on book value for its shareholders year in, year out.

ROE starts with the surplus on trading earned for shareholders after deduction of all prior claims (interest, tax, preference dividends, minorities, etc.). This is then divided by the book value of equity on the balance sheet (after adding back any written-off or amortised goodwill or acquired intangible assets, and deducting any pure accounting items such as a revaluation reserve).

It is usual to take the average of opening and closing equity, rather than the value at the year-end; hence return on average equity or ROAE. This is because events like a large acquisition late in the year would distort the picture by boosting equity fully whilst making only a small contribution to earnings. If earnings grow faster than the increase in equity, ROE will expand, and vice versa. This was shown in Table 4.1 for DeLand and Castlefield.

DuPont Analysis

Return on equity is the product of two components: the sales-to-equity ratio and the earnings margin. Along the way, there is a whole host of variables that interact to produce that single ratio. These variables are value drivers of the business and the whole exercise is known as DuPont Analysis. It is depicted in Figure 4.2.

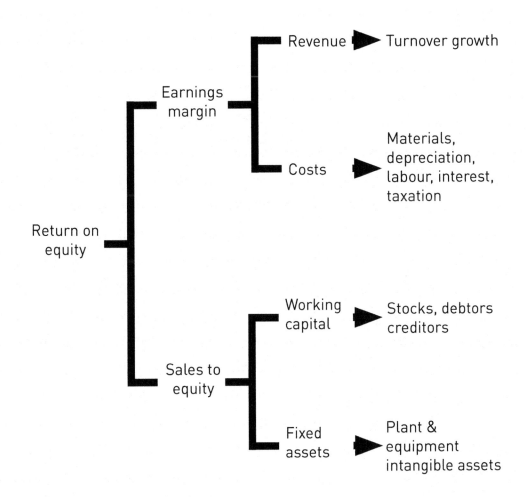

Figure 4.2 – DuPont Analysis: return on equity, value drivers tree

The **earnings margin** measures how efficiently the company and its management are converting higher sales into profit and earnings. There is an old saying that "turnover is vanity, profit is sanity" and the presence of high margins is consistent with a sane, as opposed to a vain, management. Often there will be a trade-off between sales growth and fatter margins, but the very best companies usually seem able to combine the two.

There are only two effective ways to increase the earnings margin: increase operating profit for a given level of sales or reduce the tax charge. Improving operating margins is the job of management. More gross profit can come from more aggressive pricing, keener purchasing of bought-in materials and services, and more productive labour and capital. More operating profit comes from tight control of overheads. Reductions in the tax charge can be extrinsic, such as reduced rates of business taxation, or intrinsic, like better treasury management and tax planning.

The **sales-to-equity ratio** measures how efficiently the company and its management are using the capital invested by its owners to generate higher revenues. In general, less capital tied up in assets for any given level of profit translates into less business risk and greater free cash flow.

The tree branch measures in Figure 4.2 compare fixed and working capital items to revenues. They can be influenced by company-specific or industry-specific factors. Some capital expenditure will always be required to maintain the productive capacity of the company. Still more might be required to expand the business and drive the top-line. Similarly, only a few businesses are able to grow without the need for additional working capital to finance such growth.

Both revenue profitability and capital profitability can be judged by analysis of the various ratios. I have a lot more to say on this in Chapter Eight, which deals with ratio analysis and key performance indicators.

Incremental returns on investment

The latest snapshot of how ROE is evolving comes from calculating the marginal return on the most recent slug of investment in the company. This is accomplished by dividing the incremental change in earnings by the incremental increase in equity. This is shown in the formula below, where 1 and 2 refer to consecutive years:

marginal return on equity = (earnings 2 – earnings 1) ÷ (y/e equity 2 – y/e equity 1)

What we are trying to do with the marginal return is see what effect adding more capital to the business is having on the return. There are three types of return:

1. **The total return** produced over all time by all the capital invested – a kind of historical score sheet.

2. **The average return** – the total return divided by the capital invested.

3. **The marginal return** – the incremental change in the total return resulting from the latest increment of capital added.

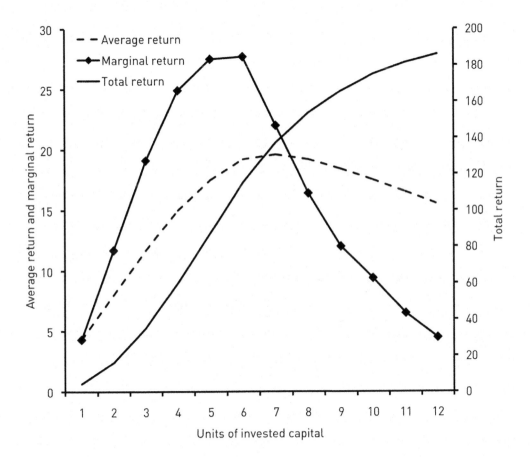

Figure 4.3 – Relationship between types of return

The relationship between the three is shown in Figure 4.3. It illustrates a very common feature of economics, namely the *law of diminishing returns*. The marginal return continues to increase until it reaches a maximum somewhere around 6 units of invested capital, whereafter it starts to decline. This peak is called the **point of diminishing marginal return**.

Crucially, the marginal return reaches its peak before the average return. As the marginal return falls back from its peak, the average return begins to flatten out. The average return will continue to rise so long as it lies below the marginal return. But once the two cross and the marginal return falls below the average return, the latter too will start to fall. Where they cross is known as the **point of diminishing average return** and, in this example, it lies somewhere between 7 and 8 units of invested capital.

The importance of analysing incremental rates of return should now be apparent. Marginal returns rise and fall long before the average and, as such, act like a magnet dragging the average up or down. They are therefore a powerful lead indicator for both the future upside and downside potential. Treated with care, they can be an early warning sign of problems lying ahead.

This is what alerted the astute investor to the situation at Rentokil described in Chapter Three. The marginal returns were moving sharply in the wrong direction and this could be seen more than six months before the profit warning.

Of course, one year's marginal returns are not always a sure-fire way of foretelling the future. New investment will usually generate a return for longer than a year and may take more than one year to build to a peak. Fortunately, there is a way to allow for this by calculating the cumulative marginal return on the extra investment put in over, say, the last three years. This introduces a smoothing factor into the analysis and may give a better representation of the trend, particularly in businesses where the immediate returns can be volatile.

What this discussion of the profitability of capital has shown is that focusing on how the balance sheet is being managed is every bit as important as focusing on the profit and loss account. Used properly, the concept of profitability of capital can help you to avoid the traps laid by companies pursuing growth for its own sake. It also explains why a narrow focus on growth alone may lead to a weak analysis.

In Chapter Five, I turn to how growth and profitability of capital can be put on an equal footing to determine exactly how much economic value is being created by a business.

CHAPTER FIVE.

Economic Profit

"Focusing on size (say earnings) could destroy value if returns on capital are low; conversely earning a high return on a low capital base may mean missed opportunities."

— COPELAND, KOLLER & MURRIN (McKINSEY & CO), 'VALUATION'

EDUCATION IS A LEARNING CURVE. YET WHERE INVESTMENT is concerned, my experience has been that the learning curve is more like a series of step jumps with each one being a point of no return. It is as though you are building a structure with the aid of a series of ladders. Having reached the next level, the search is on for the means to enable you to climb higher still.

For a long time I was stuck on one particular floor, wrestling with the trade-off between growth and profitability and how, alone or in combination, each can create value. The resolution came courtesy of the concept of economic profit. That is the subject of this chapter.

The concept of economic profit

Economic profit is defined as the profit earned by an enterprise over and above all its costs, both operational and financial, including an imputed cost to equity. It has been a part of economic theory for more than 100 years.

Economic profit is computed by taking the spread between the rate of return on the equity capital employed in a business and the imputed cost of that capital, and then multiplying the result by the economic book value of the capital committed to the business. It represents the total amount of value that is being created in a business over and above every commercial cost, including the opportunity cost of ordinary shareholders' funds.

Looked at another way, it is the interaction between the volume of equity capital that a management team is able to attract into a business and the return the management team is able to generate on this equity capital. It requires three inputs; namely growth, return on equity capital and cost of equity capital. Owing to my fixation on cash flow rather than accounting earnings, I like to add a fourth input, namely the conversion ratio of earnings to free cash.

Jerry Utton suggested a good simile for economic profit with the expansion of the Roman Empire. Growth was achieved by conquering more and more new territories, so the asset base of the empire expanded horizontally. But those territories only stayed conquered when an infrastructure was put in place that maximised their prosperity – that is, the returns on investment were maximised. Through that infrastructure, cash taxes were paid to Rome. The more extensive and the more prosperous the empire, the greater the cash flow to its owners.

If territories had been conquered and the empire had grown at the expense of depth, then plenty of productive potential would have been lost. On the other hand, if the focus had been entirely on governing, once just a few territories had been acquired and horizontal expansion had stopped, potentially productive new territories would have been overlooked. The art of developing both an extensive and a productive empire was to balance growth with productivity. As it is with empires, so it is with companies.

Calculating economic profit

There are six steps necessary to combine growth and profitability into a single measure of shareholder value creation and these are set out below. Table 5.1 gives a worked example of how to calculate economic profit for Croda International, the speciality chemicals group.

1. Compute the average gross equity capital employed in the company across any financial period. As operating profits are generated throughout a year, average gross equity is the correct denominator to use. Gross means equity shareholders' funds, plus goodwill written-off or amortised, minus revaluation reserves.

2. Take the after-tax accounting earnings in the same period.

3. Express the earnings as a percentage return on average gross equity (ROAE).

4. Subtract from that return the imputed 'cost' of using that equity capital in the business. This is equal to the return an investor might expect on the next best alternative use of his capital if it was invested in a security of the same risk class. I generally use 8% on equity, this being my 10% required hurdle rate of return on equity, less the standard corporation tax rate of 20%. (It is net of tax, because the earnings you have used to calculate returns are also net of tax.) A good analogy is that of a parent company acting as a bank to its subsidiaries and advancing a line of credit that bears interest at the cost of capital. Economic profit is the difference between the profits each unit derives from its operations and the charge for capital each unit incurs through the use of its credit line.

5. Multiply the result by the average equity in the business, which was worked out under 1 above.

6. Apply the cash conversion factor, i.e. calculate the percentage of earnings the company converts into free cash.

This is then the super-normal value that is being created for owners after they have received a normal return on their capital. With a few rare businesses, you can extend that economic profit out as an annuity.

Economic profit differs from earnings in that it is calculated after deducting a fair charge for the equity capital and it is cash-based. It will immediately show up businesses that are destroying value by growth. It will also show up businesses where returns may be coming off the boil but where the addition of more equity is producing a growing and satisfactory aggregate result. In other words, businesses that are generating more economic profit and more value for owners.

Refer to Table 5.1 and the calculation of economic profit for Croda International. The period chosen covers the landmark acquisition of Uniqema in August 2006, the great recession of 2008/9 and the movement to a much more generous dividend policy in 2010/11 following sporadic share repurchases in previous years.

It is the step change in the dividend policy that accounts for the leap in ROAE after 2010 because the equity base of the company was being depleted by the larger pay-outs to shareholders. The majority of the negative cash flow in 2007 was caused by an exceptional top-up payment of £70m in the pension scheme to reduce its deficit.

Year to December	2005	2006	2007	2008	2009	2010	2011	2012	2013	2014
Sales	305.6	518.9	804.8	956.4	916.2	1,001.9	1,028.0	1,051.9	1,077.0	1,046.6
Pre-tax profit	50.6	54.3	60.8	98.4	106.4	192.3	237.5	238.5	251.4	235.4
Earnings	32.8	36.3	40.0	66.6	71.5	129.5	162.5	164.3	178.7	169.6
Opening gross equity	141.5	132.4	177.2	270.7	316.1	209.4	326.0	319.0	397.1	466.0
Closing gross equity	132.4	177.2	270.7	316.1	209.4	326.0	319.0	397.1	466.0	535.8
Average gross equity	137.0	154.8	224.0	293.4	262.8	267.7	322.5	358.1	431.6	500.9
Return on average equity (%)	24.0	23.4	17.9	22.7	27.2	48.4	50.4	45.9	41.4	33.9
Cost of equity (%)	8.0	8.0	8.0	8.0	8.0	8.0	8.0	8.0	8.0	8.0
Spread (R-C) (%)	16.0	15.4	9.9	14.7	19.2	40.4	42.4	37.9	33.4	25.9
Economic profit (spread x average equity)	21.9	23.8	22.2	43.1	50.5	108.2	136.7	135.7	144.2	129.7
Free cash flow	36.4	17.3	(91.9)	6.0	111.0	83.1	104.4	85.9	143.6	109.4
Cash flow: earnings (%)	111.0	47.7	(229.8)	9.0	155.2	64.2	64.2	52.3	80.4	64.5
Economic cash earnings	24.3	11.3	(51.0)	3.9	78.4	69.4	87.8	70.9	115.9	83.7

Table 5.1 – Croda International plc, economic profit and economic cash earnings, 2005-2014 (£m unless stated)

The table shows how management dramatically increased economic profit almost six-fold in ten years. Whilst the economic cash earnings of the business have only risen by about 3.5 times over the same period, this is nonetheless an impressive creation of shareholder value. It is reflected in the share price performance of Croda during this time, as shown in Figure 5.1.

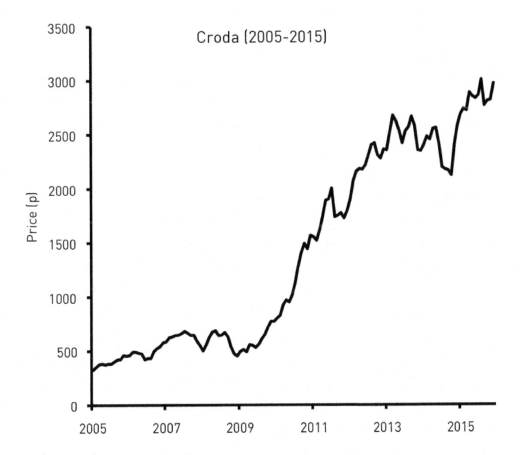

Figure 5.1 – Croda International share price, 2005-2015 (monthly average)

Growing and prolonging economic profit

The best businesses are those that grow their economic profit over extended periods of time. With that in mind, it is helpful to consider the four ways in which economic profit can be captured and expanded in any business:

1. **Improve the rate of return on the existing base of capital**. This means that higher operating profits are generated without tying up any more funds in the business. That can be achieved through products, pricing, people, customers or markets.

2. **Invest at returns that exceed the cost of capital**. Additional capital is invested in new projects that return more than the cost of obtaining the new capital. Good managers will know when they have come to the end of their stock of high returning projects; they start to return surplus capital to owners. Bad managers continue to commit capital to lower-grade projects even though they may have neither the hope nor the prospect of earning their cost of capital.

3. **Get rid of underperforming assets**. Capital is liquidated from, or further investment is curtailed in, subpar operations where inadequate returns are already being earned. Good managers will take rationalisation on the chin, knowing that investors are likely to have already discounted the accounting costs of closure or disposal and will be focusing on the likely improvement to future cash flows.

4. **Adopt a more tax-efficient capital structure**. The cost of capital is reduced by exchanging equity for tax-efficient debt.

However good the economics and management of a business, economic profit is unlikely to continue to grow indefinitely. There is a finite time period over which investors can expect management to initiate new, value-adding projects, either internally through organic means, or externally via acquisitions.

Over time, what usually drives economic profit down is either new entrants into a market, attracted by the size of returns being generated by existing players, or substitute products that reconfigure the product proposition. Think of the market for horse-drawn carriages that changed forever after Henry Ford set up in business or how Hoover was a generic and dominant name for vacuum cleaners for generations, until James Dyson came along.

Economic profit is more likely to be prolonged in simple businesses that are expertly managed, rather than in businesses that depend on a technical edge prone to be eroded by a maverick competitor who couldn't care less about immediate returns on his capital.

Market value-added

Market value-added is closely related to economic profit. The two concepts work hand in hand in establishing what true value a business has created, what that value is worth and how it is being priced by the stock market.

The measure is the total market value-added to a company by investors over and above its net asset value. That is, the market value of the equity less all the share capital that has been invested in the business since day one. What it represents is the market's present value expectation of all the economic profit that will be added to the business in the future through its participation in successful projects. What 'earnings' is to 'market capitalisation', 'economic profit (EP)' is to 'market value-added (MVA)'. The key difference is that the EP/MVA relationship eliminates capital and the cost of capital and focuses solely on super-normal value creation.

The stock market only prices a business above its net asset value if it believes the business can earn superior rates of return on its future stream of projects. Assume that the equity capital invested in a business can be turned into cash and that the cash could earn the risk-free deposit rate of return – let's say 5% in normal times. If the company was in fact earning business returns of 20% on that capital, you might be prepared to pay close to four times its net asset value to participate in a 5% annuity.

If you paid £3.50 in the market for £1 book value of capital, for example, your return would be 5.7% (20% on £1 ÷ £3.5). If you paid £2.50, that return would increase to 8% (20% on £1 ÷ £2.5). The difference between what you are prepared to pay to participate in an income stream and the original book value of capital invested to get it is the market value-added. In the latter example, market value-added would be £1.50 (£2.50 - £1.00).

Businesses that are capable of earning more than their cost of capital produce positive economic profit and build premiums into their market values. The ones that earn superior returns are usually those supplying differentiated or niche products and services and, of course, those that are efficiently run. Often, the configuration of a businesses' cost structure and the way it is set up are vital determinants of its ability to create economic profit, as is its potential to scale up. Massive economic profit has been created by businesses like Microsoft, Google and Apple because of their proprietary configurations and their international scalability.

Businesses that fall short of investors' required rates of return generate negative economic profit and they see the stock market discount the value of the capital they employ. They are usually to be found in commodity-type products and services. They often fail to reach their cost of capital because competitive entry is relatively easy and rivalry can be intense, putting profitability under pressure.

Spotting value anomalies

Economic profit can be a very valuable tool with which to spot anomalies in company valuations. Because it consists of two parts – the amount of capital invested and the rate of return on that capital – you can isolate either or both of these variables with a view to determining value.

Reckitt Benckiser

Take a company that has been earning a relatively pedestrian return on its capital employed in the past but, through the influx of new management, now proposes to acquire a business that has strong growth potential and high returns to investment (and better still, the incoming business uses little capital to expand value). This is what happened when Bart Becht joined the board of Reckitt & Colman in December 1999 on the acquisition of Benckiser NV, a business operating in a similar field to Reckitt but with a vastly superior operating performance.

With businesses that have little need for fixed or working capital, owner value can be added very quickly. Smart management may use debt to acquire the incoming business and expense away the cost over time, i.e. they use operational cash flow to repay all the money it borrowed to finance it.

Becht added huge economic profit to Reckitt Benckiser very quickly. The year after he became CEO, the company reported sales of £3,133m, pre-tax profits of £447m and earnings of £314m. By 2005, these metrics had grown to £4,179m, £876m and £669m respectively. In 2010, the year before his retirement, sales had reached £8,453m, profits £2,231m and earnings £1,661m. Making the same calculation as for Croda in Table 5.1, return on average equity increased from 17.5% through 27.0% to 31.4%. In turn, this meant that economic profit over the period had risen over seven-fold from £171m to £1,237m.

It is hardly surprising, therefore, that Reckitt Benckiser was the fourth best performing share in the FTSE 100 Index during this time. Figure 5.2 captures this dramatic share price performance.

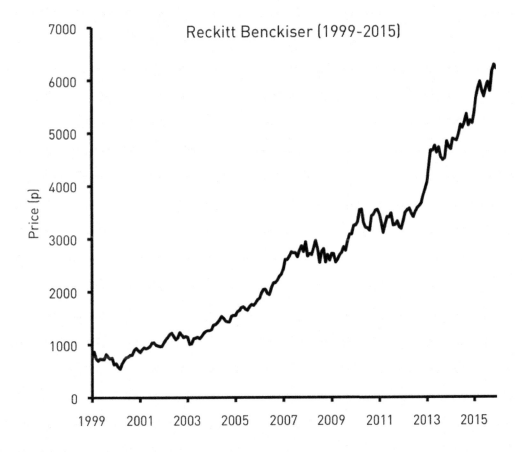

Figure 5.2 – Reckitt Benckiser share price, 1999-2015 (monthly average)

Sage Group

Investors frequently believe that the stock market has it right all the time and opportunities for profit are limited. Nothing could be further from the truth, as the following example of the madness of crowds shows.

Near the end of the dot-com boom, the stock market value of Sage Group's software business over and above its net assets, that is the market value-added, increased by £2.2bn in one year alone (1999). The starting point for the economic profit reflected in that mind-boggling monetary anticipation was an increase of £7.5m on the previous year, a yield of just 0.3%. Incremental economic cash earnings were less still – just £5m on the strength of a 67% conversion rate to cash from reported earnings. Just to reach the point at which the economic profit yield became a reasonable 5% EP/MVA yield, earnings, net of the cost of capital, would have had to reach £110m – nearly 15 times the starting level.

A simple bit of economic profit analysis would have told you that this was an investment proposition made in Hell and strictly for the insane. If you were a Sage investor, that 0.3% EP/MVA relationship was going to come to a pretty dramatic and painful end (see Figure 5.3). No wonder Buffett, referring generally to the dot-com boom, was moved to declare in May 2000: "There is no question in the last year, the ability to monetise shareholder ignorance has ever been exceeded."

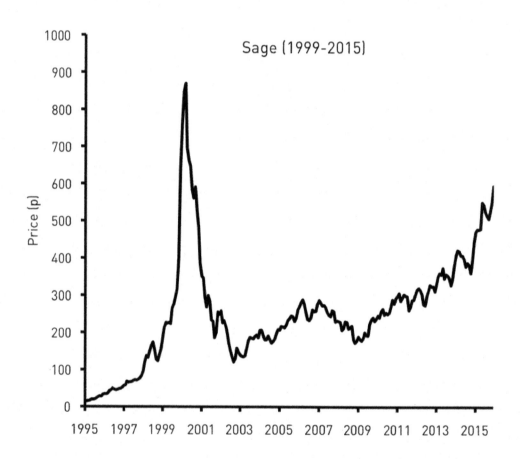

Figure 5.3 – Sage Group share price, 1995-2015 (monthly average)

The main takeaway point is that mastering economic profit and its relationship with market value-added keeps you from allocating capital to investments that have neither the hope nor the prospect of providing you with a decent return on your capital.

I have already touched on the importance of seeing earnings reflected in cash flow when discussing the calculation of economic cash earnings. Chapter Six is devoted to explaining why conversion of a high level of earnings into free cash is not only desirable but an essential component of company analysis.

CHAPTER SIX.
Cash Is King

"We get suspicious when a business reports profits without generating cash."

– LORD ARNOLD WEINSTOCK

I F THERE IS ONE CHAPTER OF THIS BOOK – AND ONLY ONE chapter – that investors should read, understand and commit to memory, this is it. In 'Cash Is King', I look at the various factors that can influence cash generation and how cash flow can diverge so sharply from what a company might be reporting in profits. Learn these lessons and you will seldom go far astray.

In October 1974, the *Wall Street Journal* published the following critique. It encapsulated the blind faith in earnings per share growth as the key determinant of share price appreciation. It is as relevant today as it was then:

"A lot of executives apparently believe that if they can figure out a way to boost reported earnings, their stock prices will go up even if the higher earnings do not represent any underlying economic change. In other words, the executives think they are smart and the market is dumb. The market is smart. Apparently the dumb one is the corporate executive caught up in the earnings per share mystique."

Earnings, earnings, earnings

Despite empirical evidence to the contrary, this blind faith persists. There is nothing fundamentally wrong with management taking the view that earnings drive share prices. When Ben Graham in *Security Analysis* talked about the market being a short-term voting machine and a long-term weighing machine, what was being weighed was indeed earnings. The problem comes when the mystique of EPS growth results in manipulation to achieve it or where mythical earnings do not get reflected in cash.

The theoretical justification for earnings as a valuation tool is that, over time, earnings translate into cash. It was John Burr Williams in *The Theory of Investment Value* who first championed the proposition that the net present value of the stream of expected future cash flows determines the intrinsic value of an investment.

In committing to an investment, the investor gives up a scarce resource – cash. In return, he expects cash back in the future; in dividends and/or capital appreciation that can be crystallised into cash. The value of any investment is the stream of future cash flows that an investor can expect, discounted back to a lower net present value in recognition of the fact that cash received today is worth more than cash received tomorrow. "Laying out cash now to get a whole lot more cash later on," as Warren Buffett would put it.

The trouble in practice is that earnings do not always produce the cash they are supposed to. And the only earnings that count are those that get reflected in cash, either now or in the future. Earnings and their rate of growth depend to some extent on decisions taken in the finance director's office. Managers have a degree of freedom in framing what is taken into account when finalising the income statement, which then gets signed off by the auditors, giving it an aura of respectability. The difficulty is that earnings in the hands of a charlatan become as pliable as putty.

Whilst earnings are often a matter of opinion, cash is a matter of fact. Try as you might, you cannot fudge the cash position over an extended period of time without resort to fraudulent behaviour. This makes cash the ideal valuation tool. But it presents investors with a slight problem because forecasting cash movements is much more difficult than forecasting earnings, which can be smoothed. That is one reason why analysts are seduced into looking for a shorthand way, and earnings provide it.

Cash flow: the gold standard of financial analysis

When you buy a car, some new clothes, have a night out or go on holiday, you pay in hard cash. That cash comes out of your income (or earnings). However, you cannot spend your earnings as such. The only reason you equate the two is because you are used to receiving in cash what your pay cheque says you have earned in income. In fact, the cash at your disposal for consumption will not equate to anything like your earnings.

What about the travelling expenses to get to work, the cost of food, heat, light and water, property taxes and the need to maintain your home in a state of reasonable repair? All these, and more, make pre-emptive demands on your earnings and reduce your disposable income (the latter being a good proxy for free cash).

There are strong parallels in the corporate world. Here's Buffett again on the subject of cash at the 1998 Berkshire Hathaway AGM:

> "If we could see the future of every business perfectly, it wouldn't make any difference to us whether the money came from running street cars or selling software because all of the cash that came out – which is all we are measuring – between now and Judgement Day would spend the same to us ... Once it becomes distributable, all cash is the same."

And so how is it that earnings and cash flow differ markedly?

The matching principle of accounting determines that the revenues arising from a trading transaction have to be matched against all the expenses incurred in producing and delivering the goods or service to the customer.

That's fine for expenses that can be directly identified with the transaction concerned, such as raw materials or labour. But what about indirect expenses such as the establishment overhead incurred in running the business as a whole? What about recovery of manufacturing overhead or depreciation? What about apportionment of R&D expenditure? That's where the accrual principle comes in to spread costs over the period in which economic benefit is being derived from what has already been spent.

Let's now look at the five major examples of pre-emptive demands on a company's cash flow.

1. Working capital

Companies need working capital. Working capital consists of short-lived forms of asset, such as stocks and work-in-progress, debtors and creditors. The formula is:

net working capital = stocks + debtors – creditors

Input factors, such as raw materials and consumables, are converted into finished goods and services for sale. Stocks and work-in-progress represent costs incurred in a given accounting period by having added value to the input factors. These costs are carried over into the next period because the goods have yet to be sold and therefore the costs cannot yet be matched against revenue.

Debtors (also known as receivables) represent credit granted to the customers of the business – in other words money owed to the company that has yet to be collected. The accrual concept of accounting demands that revenues and their costs be married up. Goods and services delivered and invoiced, but yet to be paid for, are recognised in turnover and the consideration outstanding initially goes into the balance sheet as a debtor under current assets. Only when the customer pays up does the amount come out of the debtor ledger and go into the cash balance. Until the customer pays, the profit has been recognised but the cash has yet to be received.

As long as the stocks can be sold, and the debtors collected, all we are dealing with here is a timing difference. The problems arise when obsolescence sets in, leaving unsold inventory on the shelves, or customers fail to pay their debts. Converting these stocks and debtors into cash is then fraught and usually calls for write-downs or write-offs. In the process, cash is sacrificed.

Companies are sometimes tempted to go for growth by granting more favourable terms of trade to their customers, i.e. allowing them a longer time to pay. Tell-tale signs of this are systematic increases in the ratio of working capital to sales (in other words, how much working capital is supporting each £1 of revenues) and lengthening trade debtor days.

Creditors and accruals (also known as payables) represent credit received by the company, i.e. money owed by the company for economic benefits already obtained, but which have yet to be paid for. They are high ranking claims on future cash flow. Similarly, deferred income is money already received or due, which has yet to be earned by the company through the provision of matched goods or services, e.g. maintenance contract income or subscription income.

Over time, the requirement to invest in additional working capital should be a reflection of growth and it should rise roughly in line with turnover. This is not always the case, however. The absorption of cash into working capital is the most frequent cause of divergence between what a company reports in profits and what it generates in cash.

2. Capital expenditure and depreciation

A company might buy a machine that is expected to produce goods for ten years before it needs replacement. The economic cost of the machine to the company is therefore spread over ten years' production. Obviously the capital cost of this machine should be apportioned over the ten-year period and not solely in the year it was bought. This is done by charging a depreciation provision in each year.

The problem here is the leeway given to management to determine both the mechanics of how this charge is made and the estimate of residual value that the capital asset will have at the end of its useful life. Such decisions have an impact on reported profits.

There are several methods of charging depreciation, the more common of which are:

1. **Straight-line** – the usual method employed. Here the charge is spread equally over the useful economic life. If the machine cost £100,000, has an expected life of ten years and an expected residual value of £20,000, then the annual depreciation charged against income is: (£100,000 - £20,000) ÷ 10 = £8,000 per annum.

2. **Declining or reducing balance** – this is the method often used to determine the tax liability. Here the annual charge represents a fixed percentage of the remaining net book value (i.e. original cost less aggregate depreciation). In our example, the depreciation rate required to reduce the book value of the machine to £20,000 over ten years is 14.866%. In this case, the annual depreciation charge starts out at £14,866 in year one, falling to £3,492 in year ten.

3. **Sum of the years' digits** – this is the method sometimes used for leasing activities where there is a heavy capex in early years. Here the cost less residual value is divided by the sum of the years' digits to give a unit of depreciation. The first year is charged with ten units, the second with nine units and so on to the tenth year with one unit. Thus in our example, one unit of depreciation is £80,000 ÷ (the sum of 1 to 10) = £80,000 ÷ 55 = £1,455. The annual charges then start off as £14,550 in year one falling to £1,455 in year ten.

Since depreciation is charged against profits, adopting method (1) in preference to methods (2) or (3) will lead to reporting higher profits in the early years. However, the key point to take on board is that there is no effect on cash flow because the money went out in year one and was recorded as a purchase of fixed assets in the year one cash flow statement. No additional money goes out with the depreciation provisions in years two to ten. We can see immediately that the profit record has diverged from the cash record.

The machine might be sold at some point for a consideration different to its net book value. If it is sold for above net book value, the profit and loss account will have been charged with too much depreciation and it has to be credited with a balancing gain; if it is sold below net book value, there will be a balancing loss to record. But again, the cash flow statement avoids this by recording only the cash received for the machine as a sale of fixed assets in the year when the disposal was made.

3. Capitalised expenditure

Capitalised expenditure might be assets under construction, e.g. new buildings, or R&D expenditure where the economic benefits are expected to accrue in future years, e.g. software development or bringing a new drug to market.

In the case of the former, the assets under construction will be transferred to tangible fixed assets once the building programme is completed. In the case of the latter, there is much more leeway. Management can choose to write off R&D as incurred (the most prudent way), or it can capitalise it and then amortise it over the period during which economic benefits are expected to arise. This is fine so long as the R&D proves fruitful. But what if the benefits don't accrue as expected or there are performance-related problems? The cash has been spent.

It was the money spent (and the subsequent need to write-off capitalised development expenditure) on the RB211 aero engine that caused Rolls-Royce to go bust and have to be rescued by the government in 1971.

4. Acquisitions

When one company is acquired by another, the assets purchased will have a net book value but the acquiring company may amend this upon consolidation. Adjustments can be made to align accounting policies or assets can be written down to reflect what the acquirer considers to be realisable value. Provisions may be set up to cover integration and rationalisation costs. Together these items are referred to as fair value adjustments and they are a rich source of smoke-and-mirrors accounting.

Written down fixed assets reduce the depreciation charge to the income statement over the remaining life of the acquired assets. Stocks may be sold later at a price higher than the written down value. Provisions made for doubtful debts might not be needed. In each event, post-acquisition profits would be inflated. However, cash flow is unchanged because the money goes out on day one as consideration for the assets acquired.

What is happening is that the balance sheet takes the initial hit but subsequent profits are inflated. These then rebuild the balance sheet as they come back in the form of retained earnings. As new stocks bought at current prices and new debtors at full valuation take the place of ones written-down on acquisition, there appears to be an increase in assets. In both cases, working capital increases.

Likewise, integration and reorganisation provisions are a technique for making such costs appear as exceptional items in the income statement, with the invitation to regard them as one-off items to be excluded from adjusted profits. But items such as redundancy payments – which commonly have this treatment applied to them – are a cash cost to the company. Excluding them means that adjusted profits provide an overoptimistic assessment of the true cash performance of the company. I have always argued that integration costs are part and parcel of an acquisitive company's real expenses, so they should not be hidden under the carpet.

The excess over net book value paid by a company when acquiring the business of another is termed (accounting) goodwill. Prior to 1998, goodwill was immediately extinguished against reserves. From then on until the implementation of International Financial Reporting Standards (IFRS) in the mid-2000s, it was capitalised and amortised through the income statement over a maximum of 20 years. Nowadays, it remains on the books as an intangible asset unless an impairment test shows that there has been a diminution in its value, in which case it is written-off.

What this means, in practice, is that companies that were frequent acquirers of other businesses prior to the implementation of IFRS will have the book value of their assets, and hence net equity, artificially lowered by goodwill written-off to reserves or amortised. Hence the reason I always add back goodwill written-off or amortised to shareholder equity when analysing a company's accounts. For the same reason, I deduct revaluation reserves, which inflate equity by revaluing upwards land and buildings from cost to market value.

Like depreciation and gains or losses on the sale of fixed assets, amortisation is added back to operating profits when reconciling them to operational cash flow. But unlike depreciation, goodwill amortisation is not an economic cost to the acquiring company. At the end of the arbitrary 20 or whatever years, the acquisition does not have to be replaced (though the tangible assets acquired probably will have been replaced along the way). In fact, if the franchise is well managed, economic goodwill (as opposed to accounting goodwill) should build over time.

A similar adjustment as for a sale of surplus fixed assets is made for a business disposal, which might generate a gain or loss over book value. The cash flow statement records the cash received as a result of the divestment; any gains or losses are removed from profits.

5. Interest and taxes

Interest shown in the income statement is that receivable or payable during the accounting period. The figure does not record what is actually received or paid – this appears in the cash flow statement. Similarly, the tax charge in the income statement is that accrued during the accounting period: that shown in the cash flow statement is what has actually been paid.

Other than simple timing differences on collection, the three most common causes of discrepancies are:

1. **Loan arrangement fees to banks**. These are paid at the point of inception but it is usual to amortise such fees over the term of the new loan. Thus the income statement is only charged with a portion of the fee in each year, whereas the entire amount will have been a cash outflow in year one.

2. **Defined benefit pension schemes**. As a result of new accounting standards that came in with IFRS, scheme surpluses and deficits have to be shown on the balance sheet. The income statement is charged or credited with the expected return on the scheme assets less an imputed interest charge on the liabilities. This is purely an accounting item. The true cash cost to the company is the normal employer contribution to the scheme plus any top-up charges to reduce a scheme's underfunding. These are taken through the cash flow statement.

3. **Deferred tax**. This is a provision that results from HMRC granting allowances against corporation tax for capital expenditure. It is the divergence between what a company is actually liable to pay on taxable trading profits and what would have been payable had the capital allowances equaled the annual depreciation charge. As long as the company does not cut back heavily on

capital expenditure, the liability is unlikely to crystallise. It is a provision, not a cash tax, and has no effect on cash flow.

What these five examples demonstrate is that there are many good reasons to concentrate as much, if not more, on the cash flow statement than the profit and loss account.

The various measures of cash flow

Investment bankers and analysts talk a lot of rubbish about cash flow. For example, trying to value a company by the amount of gross cash flow it generates is particularly daft. The measure in question is the so-called EBITDA metric (earnings before interest, tax, depreciation and amortisation). Interest and taxes have to be paid if the company owing them is not to be foreclosed upon and depreciation is a true economic cost to the business – a replacement provision for worn-out productive assets.

Any business reliant upon significant productive fixed assets always has an attendant requirement to invest cash in them just to remain competitive in terms of unit sales. Therefore, to rely on a figure that is stated before a requirement just to stay in business is nonsense.

The corporate world likewise prefers to show its operational cash flow as a key performance indicator – particularly when measured against operating profit. Operational cash flow is operating profit plus non-cash trading items, such as depreciation and amortisation, plus or minus working capital movements. Again, this is not particularly intellectually rigorous. In adding back depreciation to profits, no corresponding and symmetrical charge is made for capital expenditure, which is the cash flow partner of depreciation. This seems to me irrational.

My preference – and indeed that of most serious observers without either an axe to grind or a favourable investment case to dress up – is to use free cash flow. This is defined as follows:

free cash flow =
operational cash flow ± interest received or paid – cash taxes – net capex

The natural profit and loss measure to compare this with is earnings attributable to shareholders, i.e. profit after tax, minorities and preference dividend payments.

Of course, capital expenditure can take one of two forms. Maintenance capex is that necessary to replace worn-out fixed assets, which must be maintained to keep the existing operations in good order. Expansion capex is often held to be discretionary investment made with the intention of supporting future growth of revenues, earnings and cash flow.

There is no hard line between the two and, personally, I don't buy into the argument that most expansion capex is discretionary. Usually, I think nearly all capex is required to maintain the company's competitive position. Where I am prepared to concede possible exceptions to this is in cases such as JD Wetherspoon opening new pubs or Lavendon Group investing in additional plant to hire out. Then the depreciation charge is probably a better approximation of the maintenance capex requirement of the business. In this case, the cash flow metric is better described as cash earnings to make the distinction between it and free cash flow.

Earnings but no cash: the demise of Finelist Group plc

I mentioned in Chapter One the fate of many of the 1980s mini-conglomerates who elevated the manufacture of apparent earnings growth through acquisitions into an art form. Their destiny confirmed the old adage that 'no company generating plenty of cash ever goes bust, which cannot be said for companies generating plenty of profit'. In 1998, I was able to apply what I had learned ten years earlier to a more recent exponent of acquisition accounting. The company in question was Finelist Group and, like Rentokil, the prognosis was pretty clear.

Background

Finelist was established in 1991 and made its stock market debut three years later. Thereafter it set about consolidating the UK vehicle parts aftermarket with a vengeance. This resulted in a plethora of acquisitions and a rapid expansion of turnover and profits as the new subsidiaries were digested. Between 1996 and 1998, the already frenetic pace of acquisition activity shifted up a gear.

Boosted by acquisitions, headline turnover growth had been phenomenal, averaging 89% compound per annum between 1993 and 1998. Finelist had also turned in compound annual EPS growth of 61% in this time, which underscored its perception as a growth stock.

However, when compared with cash flow, this earnings performance begged some serious questions. Operational cash flow had fallen materially short of operating profits in five of those six years. Set against aggregate reported earnings of £45.4m, Finelist generated only £12.3m of free cash, meaning that cash averaged less than 30% of profits during this period of strong growth. This free cash was barely enough to cover £11.8m of equity dividends paid and meant that acquisition financing came from either raising fresh equity or borrowing from the bank. The cash flow and debt statistics are set out in Table 6.1.

Year to June	1993	1994	1995	1996	1997	1998
(a) Operational cash flow:						
Operating profit	1.2	2.6	7.9	9.2	20.6	35.4
Depreciation	0.1	0.3	1.0	0.9	2.4	4.8
Other trading adjustments	-	(0.1)	0.6	(0.2)	(0.2)	1.6
Gross cash flow	1.3	2.8	9.5	9.9	22.8	41.8
Net interest paid	(0.3)	(0.4)	(0.7)	(0.7)	(2.1)	(5.5)
Cash taxes paid	(0.3)	(0.3)	(0.8)	(2.0)	(4.2)	(4.4)
Net cash flow	0.7	2.1	8.0	7.2	16.5	31.9
(b) Investment cash flow:						
Working capital	(0.5)	(1.5)	(1.1)	(4.7)	(13.6)	(20.0)
Capital expenditure	(0.2)	(0.4)	(1.2)	(2.4)	(4.6)	(9.0)
Sale of surplus fixed assets	0.2	0.1	0.5	0.9	0.8	2.6
Free cash flow	0.2	0.3	6.2	1.0	(0.9)	5.5
Acquisitions	(0.4)	(0.4)	(21.6)	(3.9)	(97.3)	(108.4)
Post-expansion cash flow	(0.2)	(0.1)	(15.4)	(2.9)	(98.2)	(102.9)
Reported earnings	0.4	1.4	4.8	5.8	13.3	19.7
Free cash flow: earnings (%)	52	22	127	18	-7	28
(c) Financial cash flow:						
Dividends	-	-	(0.9)	(1.8)	(2.6)	(6.5)
New equity issued	-	3.3	12.4	-	77.2	0.3
Closing net cash (debt)	(1.8)	1.2	(4.4)	(9.1)	(37.7)	(156.9)

Table 6.1 – Finelist Group plc, cash generation and debt, 1993-1998 (£m unless stated)

Analysis

Management argued the need to invest in fixed and working capital in under-invested acquired subsidiaries. This may have been so, but it still constituted a demand on shareholder cash. Also, when absorbing an acquisition, Finelist invariably set up fair value adjustments to the target's assets and liabilities before bringing them onto its own balance sheet.

There had been some very large movements going on in these balances immediately prior to consolidation. For example, in 1997 over £9.8m of fair value adjustments were made, reducing the carrying value of the assets acquired by almost 30%. Asset write-downs or provisioning for liabilities increased the goodwill element relating to the acquisition which, of course, depressed shareholders' funds.

A higher working capital requirement was the main reason for Finelist's poor operational cash flow; less material was a low depreciation charge in relation to the operating flows of the business. Over those six hyperactive years, additional working capital had absorbed £41.4m of cash. Including that assimilated through acquisitions, the increase in working capital during 1998 was 161% compared to turnover growth of 70%. The same applied to previous years: 1997: 192% -v- 112%; 1996: 25% -v- 10%; 1995: 466% -v- 307%; 1994: 73% -v- 50%. This was systematic.

Acquisitions spending between 1995 and 1998 totalled £231.2m. Related equity issues raised £89.8m of this, net of expenses. With no contribution from internally generated cash, this meant that higher indebtedness filled the void. Finelist went from net cash of £1.2m as at end June 1994 to net borrowings of £156.9m as at end June 1998, representing gearing of 228%. This high level of debt was worrying because on past performance it was difficult to see how it could be paid down without resort to another rights issue.

There were other aspects of the balance sheet that gave cause for concern too. Net working capital to sales had been consistently escalating as the stock turn fell, despite Finelist appearing to take longer credit from suppliers. Shareholders' funds were substantially reduced by £129.7m of goodwill set off against reserves. Adding back this sum, gross shareholders' funds stood at £247m. Of this, retained profits constituted only 34%.

Furthermore, returns on capital and equity were faltering. Taking the average figures, adjusted for the goodwill written-off, ROCE fell from 45.4% in 1994 to 12% in 1998, whilst the more important ROE measure fell from 30.4% to 10.4%. Earnings in 1998 were £19.7m, an excess of £18.3m over 1994. This excess represents a return of only 7.6% on the £240.3m of incremental equity raised or retained during this time. No wonder the ROE went down so much. It suggested that no economic value was being added from all the frenetic acquisition activity. Finelist was having to run hard to stand still.

Epilogue

What really beggars belief is that the analysts who covered the company, supposedly intelligent guys, continued to laud Finelist for the quick-fire series of deals being done. Buy, buy, buy they wrote. Why could they not see the car crash coming? My contention is that most everyone else was hung up on the mystique of EPS growth. Just look at Table 6.1 again. Here are some additional points that were blindingly obvious:

- Cash taxes are paid out on book operating profit – if the operating profit is a cash fiction then this substantially worsens things for the business. The profit on which cash taxes are levied is in itself a cash fairy tale. Cash interest payable is the same issue – the operating profits may not be there in cash. Both the cash and the taxes then become mandatory cash outflows.

- Working capital was taking more and more of the gross cash flow and free cash flow was static or declining.

- Acquisitions would most likely have the same cash shape as the fundamental business, so Finelist was piling up layer upon layer of cash-absorbing activity every time it did a deal. Much of the £108.4m spent on acquisitions in 1998 was paid in cash, yet no cash was coming back from those deals. In fact, they would have been absorbing cash. So the more acquisitive the group was, the worse the problem got.

- By borrowing to fund part or all of the acquisition costs, another dose of toxicity was laid on the shareholders; interest to pay and principal to repay to the banks geared to operating profits – all to come out of more and more businesses that were generating no cash whatsoever.

Finelist soldiered on for around another two years after all this. During this time it failed to cement a merger with rival Partco and, starved of access to new capital, was forced to put into reverse the acquisitions strategy. Swathes of the business were sold off to contain, let alone reduce, debt levels. A bid approach in early 2000 came to nothing and in October of that year, Ernst & Young were appointed administrative receivers to the company. The company whose logo was a flying swan had been brought back down to earth with a bump.

The conclusions to draw from this sorry story are simple. Firstly, the only earnings that count are those that get reflected in cash, either now or in the future. Secondly, the value of any investment is governed by the stream of future free cash flows that an investor can expect, discounted back to present value in recognition of the fact that cash received today is worth more than cash received tomorrow. This is what ultimately drives the share price and provides you with your capital appreciation. Thirdly, by focusing on the cash flow statement, rather than the profit and loss account, you can avoid the dangers of investing in companies that are long on promise and short on delivery.

Keep close the importance of cash and you won't go far wrong. It truly is the gold standard.

CHAPTER SEVEN.
Predictability And Certainty

"In this world, nothing can be said to be certain, except death and taxes."

— BENJAMIN FRANKLIN

WE KNOW FROM EXPERIENCE THAT ALL ECONOMIC activity is inherently risky, so how do you protect yourself against the possibility (some would say the probability) that you may have overestimated the economic worth of the business?

There are two factors at play here. The first is clear: buy only when there is an appropriate margin of safety between the price you pay and the value you believe you are getting. Try not to make calls that are anything other than blindingly obvious. Unless it is a no-brainer, you are best advised to stay away. It does take time for this lesson to really sink in. When it does, your record should go from good to superb.

The second is more subtle. There is a broad spectrum across which the predictability of various business models is cast. Some are predictable to a high degree of certainty – those are the ones that Business Perspective Investors prize highly – whilst others are completely the opposite and suitable only for speculators or momentum investors.

The starting point is being able to model the business financially: how does it make its money and what external factors influence its fortunes? Ask yourself how is the product used? Where does the demand come from and how reliable is that demand? Is the company providing a necessary and must-have product?

In this chapter I will explore these themes to illustrate predictability and certainty using a real-life example. I am going to use one of the best scenarios I know of how you can model a business ten or 20 years out and have the confidence that your projections afford a high degree of certainty. Let's take a look at Dignity and the economics of death.

Dignity plc

Dignity is the UK's largest provider of funeral related services. Founded in 1994, it floated on the London Stock Exchange ten years later. It has grown by consolidating the highly fragmented funeral services market, in the process garnering economies of scale.

UK demographic trends

Our starting point is an understanding of population trends. Births, deaths and marriages in the UK are recorded and published by the Office for National Statistics for England & Wales, the General Register Office for Scotland and the Northern Ireland Statistics & Research Agency.

Figure 7.1 shows the population map, or pyramid, of the UK as at mid-2014, these being the latest figures available. Clearly shown are the immediate birth spike at the conclusion of the Second World War and the subsequent baby boomer generation and its echoes.

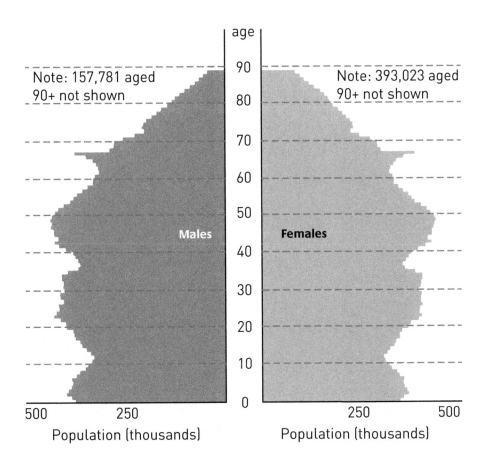

Figure 7.1 – Population pyramid by gender and age, mid-2014

Source: Office for National Statistics

The UK resident population in 2015 was 64.6m, up by 15% from 56.2m in 1974. Population growth is accelerating. In the ten years between 1985 and 1995, the population rose by an average annual rate of 0.3%. In the ten years from 1995 to 2005, population growth averaged 0.4% per annum and in the ten years from 2005 to 2015, 0.6% p.a.

In addition, the UK has an ageing population. The average age in 2014 was 40 years, an increase on 1974 when it was 33.9 years. This is the result of declines in the mortality rate and in past fertility rates. It has led to a falling proportion of the population aged 16 and under (now 19.9%) and a rising proportion aged 65 and over (now 17.7%). The comparable figures for 1974 were 26.7% and 13.8%, respectively.

In every year since 1901, with the exception of 1976, there have been more births than deaths and the population has grown due to natural change. Until the mid-1990s, this natural increase was the main driver of population growth. Since the late 1990s, however, there has still been natural increase but net immigration into the UK has been an ever more important factor in population change.

Mortality statistics

The importance of having reliable demographics is that it enables mortality projections to be prepared on the basis of assumptions regarding longevity. You know that there is a statistical probability that a given number of people are likely to die in each year. Whilst a disease epidemic or bad weather might bring forward some of the deaths, or mortals might cheat the Grim Reaper for a while, deaths will certainly occur.

Mortality statistics are also prepared by the Office for National Statistics. Figure 7.2 records the death rate in the UK since 1974 together with projections through to 2037.

The mortality rate in the UK has been falling since 1972, when it peaked at approximately 670,000. Since the turn of the millennium, this fall has gathered pace, moving down from 611,000 in 2000 to 570,000 in 2014. One notable feature, though, is the relative stability from year to year, with less than a 5% maximum annual variation in the death rate during this time.

Beyond 2016, the ONS forecasts a steady rise in the number of deaths at a compound annual rate of 1%. This is driven by the expected growth in the size of the over-60s population (the baby boomer generation).

This, then, is the macroeconomic background against which funeral services businesses operate. Importantly, it demonstrates that aggregate demand is relatively predictable.

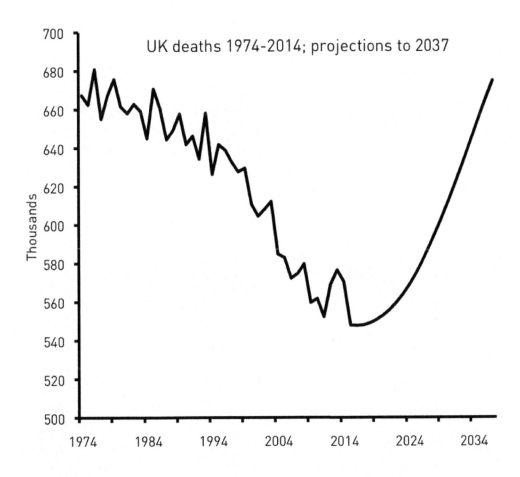

Figure 7.2 – UK deaths 1974-2014, with projections to 2037

Source: Office for National Statistics

Burials versus cremations

We also have reliable data for the relative popularity of cremations against burials. Since the first cremation was carried out in 1885, this method of disposal has gained in importance. The popularity of the practice stems from lower cost and simplicity relative to burial. However, the other two great monotheistic faiths outside of Christianity – Judaism and Islam – do not permit it. Notwithstanding, the percentage of UK deaths followed by cremation increased rapidly in the latter half of the 20th century from around 15% in 1950 to 70% in 1990. Since then, the increase has been much more modest. This is shown in Figure 7.3.

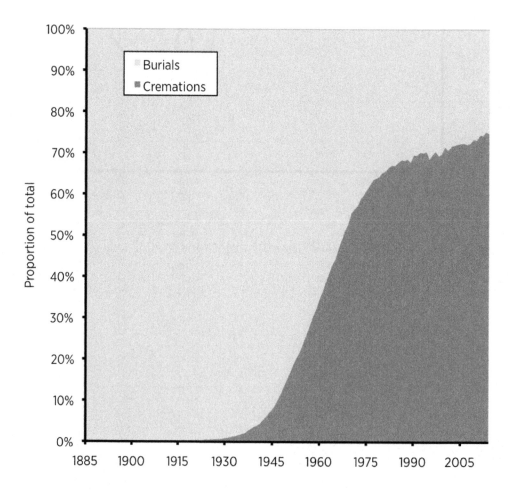

Figure 7.3 – Burials versus cremations, UK, 1885-2014

Source: The Cremation Society of Great Britain

Revenue model

Dignity has three discrete income streams: funeral services derived from its estate of funeral homes; crematoria operating in several locations; and pre-arranged funeral plans sold mainly through affinity partners but also in Dignity funeral homes.

Funeral services income comes from the fees paid to the funeral director for direct services and co-ordinating indirect services provided by doctors, clergy and the managers of cemeteries and crematoria. Crematoria turnover comes from the fees generated from Dignity's privately owned or contract operated crematoria. The services include cremation of the deceased, use of the adjoining chapel, collection, scattering or interment of the ashes and securing Home Office permissions. For burials and cremations, additional services such as the sale of memorials and plots are available at extra cost.

On top of this there is the revenue derived from the sale of pre-arranged funeral plans taken out to cover the cost of a funeral before the plan holder dies. These insurance policies are sold mainly through affinity partners but also in Dignity funeral homes.

Each income stream can be modelled using the industry data displayed in Figures 7.1 to 7.3. Here's how.

Funeral services

In 2014, the group carried out 65,600 funerals, giving it a market share of 11.8% of the 555,700 estimated total deaths in Great Britain. (We exclude Northern Ireland because Dignity has only a small presence in the province.) This activity generated turnover of £184.4m and a contribution to operating profit of £66.3m.

The estate of 718 funeral homes is widely dispersed throughout Great Britain. The typical Dignity location undertakes 130 to 140 funerals per year, with the smallest carrying out fewer than 100 funerals to the largest performing 800 to 900 funerals each year. The breadth of Dignity's portfolio introduces an element of stability into the income stream.

A single site might experience as much as a ±15% annual swing in the number of funerals performed, but by having this diversified network of funeral homes and an overall market share approaching 12%, Dignity's performance tends to track the national pattern. This shows a much lower annual variation. In the last 40 years, the highest up-year has been +4.0% (1985) and the lowest down-year -4.9% (1994), with 26 moving by less than ±2%.

Whilst there is a natural tendency to lose a little market share over time at each location, this is compensated for by acquiring new funeral homes. Net of closures, Dignity has added 206 new locations in the last ten years, either by acquisition or start-up. This has taken the estate from 512 homes to 718.

Regarding sales, Dignity derives a high proportion of revenue from complementary higher value-added activities such as providing flowers, memorials, caskets and urns. The increase in the average price of a Dignity funeral from £1322 in 2001 to £2811 in 2014 represents a compound annual growth rate of 6%. This was helpful at a time when death rates were falling, but beyond 2016 rising mortality is set to become another driver of growth.

Knowing mortality projections, likely market share and historic funeral cost inflation enables turnover to be estimated with some degree of certainty – right through to 2037 where the ONS projections stop.

Being a consolidator in a fragmented industry, Dignity has the potential to improve margins through economies of scale. Operating margin has risen gently from 30% to over 36% in the space of ten years as the larger estate generates greater revenues spread over relatively fixed central costs. It is then a small step to estimate the projected profit contribution.

Crematoria

As we have seen, cremations currently account for some 75% of all funerals performed in the UK. Dignity owns or operates 39 of the 245 crematoria in operation. In 2014, it performed 53,400 cremations out of 429,300 nationwide, giving it a market share of around 12.4%. The increase in the average price of a Dignity cremation over the same period of 2001 to 2014 has been from £483 to £1034, again representing a compound annual growth rate of 6%.

The trading margin earned on crematoria revenues has been relatively stable and comfortably in excess of 50% in recent years. So once again we have the macro projections, market share, cost and margin data needed to project well out into the future.

Pre-arranged funeral plans

Money is invested by an independent trust fund in low-risk securities to generate sufficient returns to offset future funeral services cost inflation. Dignity keeps around 20% of the premium to cover its marketing and administration expenses.

If sold by a partner, Dignity will give up 85-90% of this and book the remaining 10-15% as profit.

Historically, Dignity has performed three-quarters of the funerals covered by these plans. Outstanding plans are therefore akin to funerals in the pipeline. The number of unfulfilled plans in existence has climbed steadily from 144,600 at the end of 2001 to 348,000 at the end of 2014.

In any one year, around 6% of living plan-holders will die. Typically Dignity will sell about 25,000 net new plans each year with the average revenue generated per plan rising at about £10-15 per annum. This makes it a relatively simple task to model the division's revenues and apply an appropriate contribution margin to determine the profit.

Capital structure

Such predictable cash flows have enabled Dignity to go for whole business securitisation. The issue of Loan Notes secured on the business means that interest costs have been fixed whilst the principal and interest amortise fully over their life. A refinancing in 2014 means that there are currently two classes of Loan Notes in issue:

1. £238.9m of A-rated Class A Secured Notes, carrying a coupon of 3.5456% and repayable in full by December 2034; and

2. £356.4m of BBB-rated Class B Secured Notes, carrying a coupon of 4.6956% and repayable in full by December 2049.

By issuing Secured Loan Notes, Dignity has fixed its interest costs whilst the principal and interest amortise fully over the lifetime of the instruments. The debt issue costs are also being amortised over the term of each class of Loan Note.

Again this is predictability to a high degree of certainty. The schedule of interest to be charged to the profit and loss account and the respective cash payments in each financial year out to 2034 are set in stone. The annual debt service obligation (principal and interest) on the Loan Notes is £33.2m, of which roughly £25m is interest at present. This represents an average cost of debt of 4.2% pre-tax, or 3.4% after the 20% UK tax shelter. That leaves only a small amount of interest to be charged on the £15.6m RBS crematorium acquisition facility and some finance leases.

To model the cash flows you have to make some other minor assumptions, for instance that working capital is not an issue, or about how much the cost of acquiring new funeral homes will rise, potential dividend increases (10% p.a.) and capital expenditure requirements. But the big numbers – revenue, contribution and interest payments on the Loan Notes – are largely predictable.

Returns of capital

Finally, we have to take into account what might happen next at the treasury level. Historically, Dignity has used cash flow to pay down debt levels and then re-gear up to five to six times EBITDA by issuing more Loan Notes of each class. The timescale for this has been every four years or so. Each time, most of the proceeds have been returned to shareholders. Allowing for accompanying share consolidations, equity shareholders coming in at the time of the flotation in 2004 have had back 324p of special dividends (plus normal dividends), set against the 230p price they paid. And they still would have 567 shares for each 1000 bought at flotation.

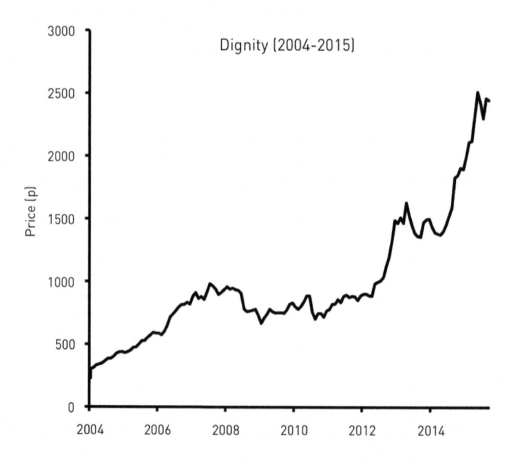

Figure 7.4 – Dignity share price, 2004-2015 (monthly average)

Figure 7.4 shows how the share price has performed in this time. This is private equity in the public arena without the burden of expensive senior and mezzanine debt.

The importance of predictability and certainty

The importance of predictability and certainty cannot be understated. As the Dignity example shows, some businesses are very simple to model (simple, though not necessarily easy) and highly predictable. You can usually tell from ratio analysis, which we go on to discuss in Chapter Eight, whether a business is stable and therefore relatively predictable.

Other examples might include NCC Group in cybersecurity, RWS Holdings in patent and commercial translation, or Unilever in branded household products. Remember, it is not what happens in any one year or two; you are investing for the long haul and need predictability and certainty to know what the business will look like in five, ten or even 20 years' time.

There is a second category of businesses that can be modelled but they are not predictable to the same degree of certainty. A third category of businesses are impossible to model in any meaningful way; if you don't know how they make their money, how can you predict with any certainty their future earnings streams?

Here is what Mary Buffett and David Clark said about the approach taken by Warren Buffett in their book *Buffettology*:

> "Warren focuses on the predictability of future earnings; and he believes that without some predictability of future earnings, any calculation of a future value is mere speculation and speculation is an invitation to folly. He will make long-term investments only in businesses whose future earnings are predictable to a high degree of certainty. The certainty of future earnings removes the element of risk from the equation and allows for a sound determination of a business's future value."

If that's good enough for the Master, then it certainly should be good enough for us.

CHAPTER EIGHT.
Ratio Analysis And Key Performance Indicators

"Most people use statistics the way a drunkard uses a lamp post, more for support than illumination."

— MARK TWAIN

IDENTIFYING TRENDS AND KEY ISSUES FROM A STUDY OF THE accounts of a business over long periods of time can be a very rewarding experience. In this chapter, I look at a suite of key performance indicators and how these are represented by various ratios. I also consider how they should be interpreted. The analysis is structured around the four main drivers of a business:

1. Sales

2. Earnings

3. Assets

4. Cash

I once again make use of worked examples, as this is the best way to illustrate the point. The main company example I use is James Halstead plc.

James Halstead plc

The turnover and profit record of James Halstead is shown in Figure 8.1.

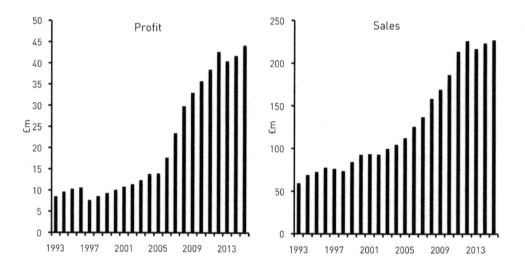

Figure 8.1 – James Halstead plc, turnover and pre-tax profit record, 1993-2015

Source: Company accounts. Figures for 1993-2006 are compiled under UK GAAP; 2007-2015 under IFRS.

Halstead manufactures and distributes branded flooring products for commercial, contract and residential markets. Eighty percent of sales come from the repair, maintenance and improvement market, rather than new-build projects. It has established a global presence on the back of innovative research.

The company has sold technically advanced products into the market for 100 years, which alone erects a high barrier to entry. Also standing in the way of would-be competitors is the enormity of the group's manufacturing facilities and the continual investment in them.

Cost control is paramount in a business like this, not least because energy costs are so large an input factor. Also important is distribution and logistics; having a network of sales agents and getting the product to the end destination on time. I dub the business 'The Crombie Overcoat of Investment' – never the height of fashion but unlikely to let you down in a storm.

1. Sales

Sales are driven by supply and demand. **Supply** is determined by:

1. The price of the product.

2. The price of the direct factors of production of the goods or services.

3. Whether the company aims to maximise revenues, by growing the market and/ or acquiring market share, or maximise profits off a given sales base.

4. The state of technology and how it might be harnessed to increase productivity.

Demand is determined by:

1. The price of the product.

2. The prices of substitute or complementary products.

3. The size of the target market's income and accumulated wealth (this being the greatest single economic factor affecting demand for the product).

4. Sociological factors like class, location, education, etc.

5. Household or company tastes depending on whether it is a business-to-consumer or business-to-business product.

The key indicator is sales per share. Ideally you want to see a minimum hurdle rate, say 5% compound annual growth, exceeded over a period of five years and the rate of growth to be accelerating or, as a minimum requirement, static. Where possible, this analysis can then be broken down into sales per product or sales by geographic area.

Next we should determine which of the main asset classes – fixed, current or human – is driving sales. Focusing on the ratios of sales to these variables will give you this information.

The suite of key sales ratios is set out in Table 8.1. In the analysis, the following definitions are used:

net working capital (NWC) = stocks + trade debtors – trade creditors

gross equity = shareholders' funds + goodwill written-off or amortised – revaluations

Year to June	2006	2007	2008	2009	2010	2011	2012	2013	2014	2015
Sales	126.0	137.3	158.7	169.3	186.4	213.9	226.3	217.1	223.5	227.3
Growth (%)	+12.2	+8.9	+15.7	+6.6	+10.1	+14.8	+5.8	-4.1	+3.0	+1.7
Sales per share (p)	62.1	67.4	77.4	82.2	90.2	103.0	109.2	105.1	108.0	109.7
Growth (%)	+11.6	+8.6	+14.7	+6.3	+9.7	+14.2	+6.0	-3.8	+2.8	+1.5
Average tangible fixed assets	19.7	18.5	19.0	22.9	26.1	29.9	32.7	32.5	32.4	31.3
Fixed asset turn	6.4x	7.4x	8.4x	7.4x	7.1x	7.2x	6.9x	6.7x	6.9x	7.3x
Average stock	19.9	21.8	27.3	29.5	32.2	42.4	50.7	54.6	57.1	58.1
Stock turn	3.4x	3.5x	3.3x	3.2x	3.3x	3.0x	2.6x	2.3x	2.3x	2.3x
Average trade debtors	17.7	18.5	19.9	21.6	24.3	28.0	29.2	29.7	32.1	31.1
Debtor turn	7.1x	7.4x	8.0x	7.8x	7.7x	7.6x	7.8x	7.3x	7.0x	7.3x
Debtor days	51	49	46	47	47	48	47	50	52	50
Average trade creditors	16.3	18.5	20.0	18.9	21.4	28.5	29.6	31.8	34.5	31.3
Creditor turn	4.2x	4.1x	4.5x	5.0x	5.0x	4.5x	4.5x	4.0x	3.8x	4.2x
Creditor days	47	49	46	41	42	49	48	53	56	50
Average NWC: Sales (%)	16.9	15.9	17.1	19.0	18.8	19.6	22.2	24.2	24.4	25.5
Average gross equity	45.3	43.4	48.8	60.1	68.8	80.5	94.3	96.8	99.0	106.8
Sales : Gross equity ratio	2.78	3.17	3.25	2.82	2.71	2.66	2.40	2.24	2.26	2.13
Average number of employees	733	779	800	777	786	811	832	829	828	838
Sales per employee (£'000)	171.9	176.2	198.4	217.8	237.2	263.8	272.0	261.9	269.9	271.2

Table 8.1 – James Halstead plc, sales ratios 2006-15 (£m unless stated)

Analysis

Figure 8.1 shows that the financial years 1996-98, 2000-02 and 2011-13 were characterised by flat revenues. Over the five years from 2010 to 2015, turnover increased from £186.4m to £227.3m, a compound annual growth rate (CAGR) of 4%. Go back ten years and the CAGR of turnover is 7.3%.

Halstead was relatively immune to the shock of the Great Recession but sales in 2013 were hit by two factors: cessation of a motorcycle accessories business (Phoenix) that turned over £6.8m in 2012 and adverse exchange rate movements.

Though a relatively mature business, the sales figures show that there is still the market opportunity and ability to grow sales above the rate of inflation. At the level of sales per share, the CAGR was 3.7% over 2010-15 and 6.9% over 2005-15.

Table 8.1 shows that the tangible fixed asset turn has been range-bound over the analysis period at 6.4 to 7.4, with the exception of a spike upwards to 8.4 in 2008. The need for a higher level of working capital to support sales is also evident. Stock turn has fallen markedly in recent years from 3.3 to 2.3, with additional stock of new products being carried at a time when sales growth experienced a hiatus.

Debt collection has remained stable, with debtor days either side of 50. Creditor days have lengthened a little, suggesting that Halstead is taking slightly longer credit from its suppliers.

In aggregate, this means that the ratio of net working capital to sales has gone up from 16.9% to 25.5% over ten years. This need for additional working capital to support sales ties up more cash on the balance sheet. Sales generated per £1 of equity invested have fallen from 278p to 213p over this period.

On the other hand, human capital has become more productive, as shown in the rise from £171,929 to £271,195 in sales per employee. This looks to have been the main driver of sales.

2. Earnings

Profitability is determined by six fundamental drivers:

1. Competition, i.e. the intensity of rivalry that exists in the market place.

2. Barriers to entry in the shape of know-how, intellectual property rights, skills, scale economies and absolute cost advantages.

3. The availability of direct and indirect substitutes.

4. The utility delivered by the products or services to their target market, thus conferring pricing power.

5. The ability to deliver that utility at an economic cost in relation to its input factors, namely materials, labour, distribution etc.

6. Control of central overheads and financial costs such as labour, property and energy costs, the rate of interest and the level of debt.

Management, systems and control are crucial also. It's no good having each of the six criteria met if management is asleep at the wheel.

Another important consideration is the stage of growth that the company finds itself in. The four stages are:

1. **Product introduction:** sales grow strongly, earnings grow more modestly.

2. **Rapid expansion:** sales grow strongly, earnings grow more strongly.

3. **Mature growth:** sales growth and earnings growth rates decline.

4. **Decline:** sales and earnings fall off.

A company with an ageing product line may appear healthy in terms of its historic growth and current profitability, but might not be able to sustain this into the future. Innovation and the introduction of better products or services then becomes the key to its growth prospects.

When analysing the past record of earnings growth, it is important to ask whether this is stable and consistent, or variable. For example, what has the record been like in periods of recession? Has the compound annual growth rate of earnings been above or below average? Has the rate of growth been static, declining or accelerating?

A company must be able to convert increasing unit sales (sales per share) into a higher rate of increase in profits and earnings. To do this it must increase its profit margins. Falling profit margins will decrease the growth rate of earnings unless sales are increasing at the same proportion to offset this.

There is often a trade-off between increasing profit margins and generating higher unit sales. The determinant is how sensitive volume demand is in relation to price changes, i.e. price elasticity. A high profit margin is good because it requires less investment in fixed, current and human assets, which, in turn, reduces business risk.

The suite of key earnings ratios for Halstead is set out in Table 8.2. Normalised pre-tax profit and earnings (profit after tax) excludes the amortisation of goodwill and exceptional items.

Year to June	2006	2007	2008	2009	2010	2011	2012	2013	2014	2015
Sales	126.0	137.3	158.7	169.3	186.4	213.9	226.3	217.1	223.5	227.3
Cost of sales	-68.5	-75.6	-90.1	-95.5	-107.0	-127.8	-133.0	-126.8	-131.8	-132.5
Gross profit	57.5	60.7	68.6	73.8	79.4	86.1	93.3	90.3	91.7	94.8
Gross margin (%)	45.6	44.2	43.2	43.6	42.6	40.2	41.2	41.6	41.0	41.7
Sales & distribution costs	-29.0	-26.3	-29.8	-31.7	-34.2	-37.9	-38.7	-39.9	-40.6	-40.7
S&D costs as % of sales	23.0	19.1	18.8	18.7	18.3	17.7	17.1	18.4	18.1	17.9
Administration expenses	-11.7	-11.8	-9.7	-9.3	-9.3	-9.9	-12.4	-9.7	-8.9	-9.4
Admin as % of sales	9.3	8.6	6.1	5.5	5.0	4.6	5.5	4.5	4.0	4.1
Operating profit	16.8	22.6	29.1	32.8	35.9	38.3	42.2	40.7	42.2	44.7
Operating margin (%)	13.3	16.5	18.3	19.4	19.2	17.9	18.7	18.7	18.9	19.7
Normalised pre-tax profit	17.7	23.5	29.9	33.0	35.8	38.5	42.7	40.5	41.8	44.2
Growth (%)	+26.7	+32.7	+27.1	+10.5	+8.3	+7.6	+11.0	-5.2	+3.1	+5.8
Tax rate on profits (%)	31.9	32.6	31.8	24.7	28.2	28.6	28.5	25.8	24.7	23.2
Normalised earnings	12.1	15.8	20.4	24.9	25.7	27.5	30.5	30.0	31.5	33.9
Growth (%)	+24.4	+31.3	+28.5	+22.1	+3.3	+7.0	+11.2	-1.6	+4.7	+7.9
Earnings margin (%)	9.6	11.5	12.8	14.7	13.8	12.8	13.5	13.8	14.1	14.9
Earnings per share [EPS] (p)	5.94	7.78	9.92	12.07	12.42	13.22	14.73	14.54	15.20	16.37
Growth (%)	+23.7	+31.0	+27.5	+21.7	+2.9	+6.5	+11.4	-1.3	+4.5	+7.7
Fully diluted EPS (p)	5.91	7.72	9.88	12.04	12.39	13.16	14.67	14.47	15.15	16.33
Growth (%)	+23.7	+30.7	+27.9	+21.9	+2.9	+6.2	+11.4	-1.3	+4.7	+7.8
Ordinary dividend per share (p)	3.06	4.13	5.19	6.06	6.69	7.15	8.00	8.75	10.00	11.00
Growth (%)	+24.1	+34.7	+25.8	+16.9	+10.3	+6.9	+11.9	+9.4	+14.3	+10.0
Special dividend per share (p)	6.25	7.50	n/a	n/a	3.75	n/a	n/a	7.00	n/a	n/a
Ordinary dividend cover	1.9x	1.9x	1.9x	2.0x	1.9x	1.8x	1.8x	1.7x	1.5x	1.5x
Retained earnings ratio (%)	48.3	46.8	47.6	49.8	46.0	45.8	45.9	39.7	34.1	32.8

Year to June	2006	2007	2008	2009	2010	2011	2012	2013	2014	2015
Average number of employees	733	779	800	777	786	811	832	829	828	838
Staff costs	22.9	25.3	26.9	28.3	30.2	31.7	32.4	32.5	33.1	33.5
Staff costs as % of sales	18.2	18.4	17.0	16.7	16.2	14.8	14.3	15.0	14.8	14.7
Op. profit per employee (£'000)	22.9	29.1	36.4	42.2	45.6	47.2	50.7	49.1	51.0	53.4

Table 8.2 – James Halstead plc earnings ratios, 2006-15 (£m unless stated)

Analysis

Figure 8.1 shows that pre-tax profit fell in 1997 and again in 2013. The former was associated with the disposal of a non-core subsidiary, Driza-Bone, in Australia, and the latter with the small dip in underlying flooring sales. Over the last five years, gross margins have been relatively stable following the decline witnessed from 2006-11. Conversely, operating margins have improved from 13.3% in 2006 to 19.7% in 2015. The reason is tight control of overheads.

Expressed as a percentage of turnover, sales and distribution costs have fallen from 23% to 17.9% and administration expenses from 9.3% to 4.1%. In addition, staff costs to sales have fallen from 18.2% to 14.7% during this period, whilst the profitability of that human capital has more than doubled from £22,913 of profit per capita to £53,365. This is consistent with a business extracting economies of scale from its growing operations.

The result is that operating profit has increased from £16.8m in 2006 to £44.7m in 2015. Over this period, the CAGR of operating profit was 11.5%, but this has slowed over the last five years to 4.5% in line with the hiatus in top-line growth.

At the level of profit after tax (earnings), the pattern is better still. Since 2006, earnings have risen from £12.1m to £33.9m, helped by reductions in UK corporation tax, which have lowered the group's effective rate of taxation from 31.9% to 23.2%. In turn, normalised fully diluted EPS have increased from 5.94p to 16.37p: a CAGR of 11.9%. The lower growth at the per-share level is due to a small increase in the number of shares in issue during this time.

Halstead has always pursued a generous dividend policy. Normal dividends have an unbroken growth record stretching back 40 years with typically between half and two-thirds of earnings paid out annually. In addition, there have been special dividends in 2005, 2006, 2007, 2010 and 2013. Over the last ten years, total dividends of £195m have been paid out of total earnings of £252.2m. This generosity is a reflection that Halstead does not need huge amounts of capital to finance its growth, so it returns the capital to its rightful owners.

3. Assets

I have already said that the strongest franchises with the greatest barriers to entry are normally reliant upon an invisible asset like proprietary technology, skill sets or owning a piece of their customers' minds. Indeed it can be argued that invisible assets are the only real source of competitive edge that can be sustained over time. Notwithstanding, in this section I am more interested in assets that can be quantified and measured, and with the returns that are being generated from those assets.

What we are looking for is how the sales, earnings and cash flow characteristics of the business are reflected in each balance sheet snapshot of assets. How are the movements in these assets developing? Are they static, declining or accelerating, and why?

Companies have a number of ways of financing their operations. The best do it internally via retained earnings, which are then reinvested at attractive rates of return. The worst do it externally by over-borrowing and/or continually passing the hat around with new share issues.

Focusing on the make-up of the assets on one side of the balance sheet and the nature of capital and reserves on the other tells you at a glance the shape of the business you are dealing with.

The key asset ratios are set out in Table 8.3. In such an analysis, goodwill would include other intangible assets acquired in business combinations such as customer lists, brand valuations, trademarks, marketing rights, etc. These are non-monetary assets without physical substance. Other definitions for terms used are as follows:

current ratio = current assets ÷ current liabilities

quick ratio = (current assets - stocks) ÷ current liabilities

gearing = net debt ÷ net equity (shareholders' funds)

Year to June	2006	2007	2008	2009	2010	2011	2012	2013	2014	2015
Net assets	42.0	39.7	49.3	62.3	66.8	85.7	94.3	90.8	98.6	106.5
Growth (%)	*-11.3*	*-5.6*	*+24.3*	*+26.3*	*+7.3*	*+28.1*	*+10.1*	*-3.8*	*+8.6*	*+8.0*
Net asset value per share (p)	8.3	7.8	9.6	12.1	12.9	16.5	18.3	17.6	19.0	20.5
Growth (%)	*-11.7*	*-6.0*	*+23.3*	*+26.3*	*+6.5*	*+27.8*	*+10.9*	*-3.8*	*+9.4*	*+7.9*
Goodwill & acquired intangible assets	3.2	3.2	3.2	3.2	3.2	3.2	3.2	3.2	3.2	3.2
Goodwill as % of net assets	*7.7*	*8.1*	*6.6*	*5.2*	*4.8*	*3.8*	*3.4*	*3.6*	*3.3*	*3.0*
Tangible fixed assets	18.7	18.3	19.7	26.1	26.1	33.6	31.7	33.4	31.4	31.2
Tangibles as % of net assets	*44.5*	*46.2*	*39.9*	*41.9*	*39.1*	*39.3*	*33.6*	*36.8*	*31.8*	*29.3*
Net current assets	33.2	22.6	34.7	43.5	48.4	56.8	65.9	64.0	76.2	86.9
Current as % of net assets	*79.1*	*57.0*	*70.4*	*69.9*	*72.4*	*65.6*	*69.9*	*70.5*	*77.3*	*81.7*
Current ratio	1.9x	1.5x	1.7x	2.1x	2.0x	2.0x	2.2x	2.0x	2.3x	2.6x
Quick (acid test) ratio	1.4x	1.0x	1.1x	1.4x	1.2x	1.1x	1.2x	1.1x	1.3x	1.5x
Net cash (debt)	25.6	19.9	29.3	27.4	33.2	33.8	38.5	34.7	38.5	47.2
Net equity	42.0	39.7	49.3	62.3	66.8	85.7	94.3	90.8	98.6	106.5
Gearing (%)	*Nil*	*Nil*	*Nil*	*Nil*	*Nil*	*Nil*	*Nil*	*Nil*	*Nil*	*Nil*
Gross equity	42.8	44.0	53.6	66.6	71.1	89.9	98.6	95.1	102.9	110.7
Growth (%)	*-10.7*	*+2.2*	*+21.9*	*+24.2*	*+6.8*	*+26.4*	*+9.7*	*-3.6*	*+8.2*	*+7.7*
Retained earnings	32.0	32.3	36.5	47.3	50.0	65.8	75.3	71.0	81.0	91.2
Retentions as % of equity (%)	*74.8*	*73.4*	*68.0*	*71.0*	*70.3*	*73.2*	*76.4*	*74.7*	*78.7*	*82.4*
Share premium account	0.3	0.8	1.7	1.7	3.0	1.1	2.0	2.1	2.7	2.9
SP account as % of equity (%)	*0.8*	*1.8*	*3.2*	*2.6*	*4.3*	*1.2*	*2.0*	*2.2*	*2.7*	*2.6*
Return on average gross equity (%)	26.6	36.5	41.7	41.4	37.3	34.1	32.4	31.0	31.8	31.8
Marginal ROE – 1 year (%)	-46.2	315.3	46.9	34.6	18.2	9.5	35.3	13.6	18.0	31.5
Marginal ROE – 3 years (%)	-38.7	-30.9	186.9	53.7	32.9	25.3	22.6	18.2	18.2	31.1

Table 8.3 – James Halstead plc, asset ratios 2006-15 (£m unless stated)

Analysis

Net assets have grown from £42m in 2006 to £106.5m in 2015, a CAGR of 10.9%, or 10.6% at the per share level. The make-up of these assets is physically strong, in the main being comprised of tangible fixed assets, of which 55% at present is freehold properties, stocks, debtors and cash. Goodwill is long standing and relates to small acquisitions made between 1999 and 2005. It represents only 3% of net assets.

On the capital side of the balance sheet, equity solidity is also strong. Retained earnings make up over 80% of gross equity, despite this having been depleted by the payment of the £195m of equity dividends in the last ten years. Conversely, the share premium account (effectively the equivalent of goodwill on this side of the balance sheet – what I call 'fresh air') is less than 3% of equity. The company carries no debt other than £0.2m of irredeemable 5.5% preference shares.

The indicators of the short-term financial position are also healthy. The current ratio has strengthened over recent years, largely as a result of the increase in cash balances. The quick ratio strips out stocks on the basis that these might not be readily saleable. In a theoretical liquidation, Halstead would comfortably be able to settle up with all its debtors and creditors, leaving its cash and other assets intact. This is evidenced by the quick ratio being well in excess of unity. The large difference between the current and quick ratios in this instance is indicative of the business carrying large levels of stock.

Return on average equity (ROAE) is the product of the sales-to-equity ratio and the earnings margin (as we saw in the DuPont analysis section in Chapter Four). The driver of ROAE has been the earnings margin, which has risen from 9.6% to 14.9% since 2006 (see Table 8.2). Concurrently, the sales-to-equity ratio has fallen from 2.78 to 2.13 (see Table 8.1). ROAE has thus risen from 26.6% in 2006 to 31.8% in 2015. The impact of paying back-to-back special dividends in 2006 and 2007 can be seen in the ROAE for 2007 and 2008, both of which exceeded 41%. The specials depleted cash and therefore shareholders' funds (equity), the denominator in the ROAE equation.

To what extent periodic returns of capital might mean that 31.8% magnifies the sustainable ROAE can be tested in two ways. Firstly, we can look at the incremental returns to equity. Over one and three years, these are remarkably close to ROAE, suggesting that this sort of quantum is sustainable.

Secondly, we can look at the operational return on assets. The sizeable cash balances generate single digit returns and lower the reported ROAE to beneath the operational (cash-adjusted) ROAE. In 2015, the average of opening and closing net cash in the balance sheet was £43.1m, whilst interest receivable was £0.2m, giving a return on cash of just 0.46%.

Net operating assets, defined as fixed assets plus stocks and debtors less creditors (i.e. excluding financial items and provisions), averaged £109.9m in 2015. Operating profit of £44.7m then produces an operational return of 40.7% on these assets.

4. Cash

The worth of a business is related to what it will earn in years to come. However, accounting earnings can be 'restricted' in the sense that what comes out in free cash is less than what is reported as earnings because of the demands of working capital and capital expenditure (capex). As we saw in Chapter Six with Finelist, a business can be reporting rising earnings that are not reflected in the cash coming out – in that case with fatal consequences.

There are a number of checks that can be made to compare the cash performance with the earnings performance. Not least is to compare the growth rate in free cash flow with that of earnings over a prolonged period. Another is the make-up of gross cash flow. Is it mainly operating profit (the best outcome), or does it rely heavily on add-backs such as depreciation or amortisation?

This then flows into a comparison of the depreciation charge against capex demands. Depreciation is nothing more than a provision for the need to replace worn out plant and machinery. Absent inflation, it therefore follows that the two measures should be similar in a static business. In a growing business, capex will often exceed depreciation. What is not acceptable is when the depreciation charge is consistently less than capex (or accumulated depreciation is less than accumulated capex). In such an instance, the reported earnings are being overstated.

The same situation applies to businesses that capitalise expenditures (usually research or development expenditure) and then dribble it back through an amortisation expense over the number of years deemed to represent the economic life of the project. Capitalisation and subsequent amortisation charge the balance sheet and not the income statement in the early years. Accounting standards provide a great amount of leeway on how these charges are treated and the finance director, whose usual interest is to report profits as high as possible, might be tempted to go for the least conservative option.

Another useful check is to look at cash interest cover. When talking of interest cover, most analysts work with the income statement. They compute how many times the gross interest *payable* is covered by operating profit plus gross interest *receivable*. But since bills are paid out of cash, a much better computation is to work with the cash flow statement and see how many times interest *paid* is covered by operational cash flow plus interest *received*.

Lastly, it is sometimes instructive to compare how cash taxes (i.e. what is actually paid over to the taxman) compare with the tax charge showing in the income statement. A difference in any single year is not remarkable; timing differences might be to blame. But if cash taxes are persistently lower than accounting taxes, it could be a sign that the taxman is seeing less profit than that showing in the accounts.

You do not want to see accounting profits persistently reabsorbed into higher working capital. This increases risk of stock not being sold, debts not being collected or obsolescence of current assets. Shareholders cannot spend working capital, only cash. Stock valuation in particular can be fudged, as can debtor balances to a lesser extent. A comparison of operating cash flow, defined as gross cash flow ± working capital changes, with operating profit is useful in this regard.

Free cash flow enables the company to reinvest in the core business that generated the free cash in the first place. Alternatively, the free cash can be deployed to buy other cash generating businesses within its core competence. Additionally, the cash can be used to retire equity, in effect meaning that the company is buying back its own business.

An interesting aside is to evaluate whether the sustainable free cash flow is enough to service the debt burden that would arise on borrowing to buy the business in its entirety. This is the first port of call for private equity buyers.

Table 8.4 sets out the key cash ratios.

Year to June	2006	2007	2008	2009	2010	2011	2012	2013	2014	2015
Operating profit	16.8	22.6	29.1	32.8	35.9	38.3	42.2	40.7	42.2	44.7
Depreciation	3.2	3.6	2.9	3.0	3.5	3.3	3.5	2.3	2.7	2.7
Other trading adjustments	-0.1	0.0	0.0	-0.9	-0.1	-0.1	-0.1	-0.1	-0.1	0.0
Gross cash flow	19.9	26.2	32.0	34.9	39.3	41.5	45.6	42.9	44.8	47.4
Interest	0.9	1.0	0.9	0.7	0.4	0.1	0.2	0.3	0.1	0.1
Cash taxes	-6.9	-8.2	-8.1	-12.8	-8.0	-9.7	-10.2	-11.3	-11.5	-8.4
Net cash flow	13.9	19.0	24.8	22.8	31.7	31.9	35.6	31.9	33.4	39.1
Working capital	5.2	0.1	-4.4	-4.3	-0.6	-8.0	-6.4	-0.2	-7.9	-4.5
Capital expenditure	-1.2	-3.5	-3.4	-9.4	-4.0	-9.7	-2.9	-3.7	-2.9	-3.8
Sale of surplus fixed assets	0.2	0.2	0.2	1.4	0.3	0.3	0.4	0.2	1.7	0.2
Free cash flow	18.1	15.8	17.2	10.5	27.4	14.5	26.7	28.2	24.3	31.0
Growth (%)	*+88.3*	*-12.9*	*+9.3*	*-38.9*	*+160.0*	*-46.9*	*+83.8*	*+5.5*	*-13.7*	*+27.3*
Free cash flow per share (p)	8.91	7.75	8.33	4.41	12.21	6.72	11.89	13.33	10.87	14.54
Growth (%)	*+90.3*	*-13.0*	*+7.4*	*-47.0*	*+176.6*	*-44.9*	*+76.9*	*+12.1*	*-18.4*	*+33.7*
Fully diluted FCF per share (p)	8.86	7.70	8.27	4.39	12.18	6.71	11.83	13.27	10.82	14.49
Growth (%)	*+90.3*	*-13.2*	*+7.4*	*-46.8*	*+177.1*	*-44.9*	*+76.5*	*+12.1*	*-18.5*	*+33.9*
Operating cash flow	25.1	26.3	27.3	29.1	36.5	32.9	37.3	42.1	35.0	42.0
Operating cash flow: op. profit	*1.5x*	*1.2x*	*0.9x*	*0.9x*	*1.0x*	*0.9x*	*0.9x*	*1.0x*	*0.8x*	*0.9x*
Cash interest cover	46.8x	77.1x	79.3x	162.4x	333.4x	310.1x	375.3x	634.9x	749.7x	879.4x
Cash taxes: accounting taxes	*1.2x*	*1.1x*	*0.9x*	*1.6x*	*0.8x*	*0.9x*	*0.8x*	*1.1x*	*1.1x*	*0.8x*
Capex: depreciation	0.4x	1.0x	1.2x	3.2x	1.1x	3.0x	0.8x	1.6x	1.1x	1.4x
Normalised earnings (£m)	12.1	15.8	20.4	24.9	25.7	27.5	30.5	30.0	31.5	33.9
Free cash flow: earnings (%)	*150*	*100*	*85*	*42*	*107*	*53*	*88*	*94*	*77*	*91*

Table 8.4 – James Halstead plc, cash ratios 2006-15 (£m, unless stated)

Analysis

The business is relatively light on tangible fixed assets, turning them 7.3 times in 2015 as we saw in Table 8.1. Accordingly, there is a modest depreciation charge that accounted for only 6% of operating profits when added back to gross cash flow. Over the last ten years, aggregate depreciation has undershot gross capex by £13.9m, with lumpy expenditures on an expansion to the warehouse in Cologne, factory extension and energy efficiency improvements at Radcliffe, the purchase and kitting out of a new warehouse at Oldham and a manufacturing facility on Teesside. The depreciation provision has provided for 69% of aggregate capex over this period.

Cash interest cover is enormous; hardly surprising given that the group operates with large cash balances and rarely uses bank facilities. There is no true debt, only the £0.2m of preference shares (which IFRS oddly treats as debt rather than permanent capital). Likewise cash taxes are comparable to the charges shown in the income statement, so no worries there.

As shown in Table 8.1, the ratio of working capital to sales has been rising steadily year-on-year as a result of higher stock levels. Possible reasons are that Halstead likes to supply homogenous product from stock to enable guaranteed 24-hour delivery and also that there has been an inventory build at Teesside. Over the last ten years, £30.9m has been absorbed into working capital, which has supported an increase in revenues of £114.9m. Thus for every £1 of incremental revenue added, the business has needed almost 27p of additional working capital to finance it, which is quite high.

Free cash generation has been generally good. Over ten years this has risen from £18.1m to £31m, a CAGR of 6.1%. At the per-share level the CAGR is 5.6%. The only years when there was poor conversion from accounting earnings were 2009 and 2011, when the capex demands of the projects referred to above had a big impact. Since these were mainly new facilities, you could argue that this is capex for expansion and future growth rather than maintenance of existing facilities and therefore unlikely to be provided by the existing depreciation charge.

Taken over the period as a whole, the aggregate conversion ratio is a satisfactory 85%. From aggregate free cash of £213.7m, ordinary and special dividends of £195m have been paid out. Net cash balances have grown from £25.5m at the start of 2006 to £47.2m at the end of 2015.

To conclude, the share price performance of James Halstead during this time is shown in Figure 8.2.

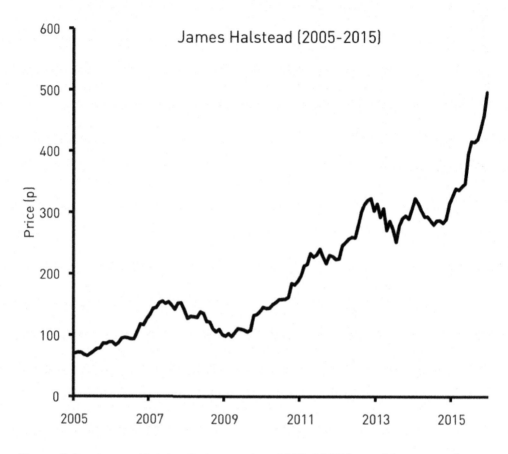

Figure 8.2 – James Halstead share price, 2005-2015 (monthly average)

Other ratios and their uses

In addition to the uses of the standard ratios covered in the Halstead analysis, other tailor-made operational ratios can be used to monitor management objectives and confirm or refute impressions. I mention just two here to give a flavour.

Games Workshop

This business designs, manufactures and sells Tolkien-esque miniature figures and the manuals used in war gaming through its owned stores, independent retailers and via mail order. Such is the hold it has on its hobbyists that I have likened it to the nearest thing to legalised drug dealing on the Stock Exchange.

Several years ago management signalled its intention to get cost out of the business by moving its owned stores from primary to secondary locations, as and when lease renewals allowed, and transitioning to one-person operations.

In 2010, the estate had an average of 382 stores whose operating lease rentals were £10.4m. In 2015, the number of stores had grown to 418 but the lease rentals had fallen to £7.6m. That means that the average operating lease rental per store had fallen from approximately £27,100 to £18,300 – with an improvement seen in each and every year. Simultaneously, sales and profit per employee rose from £61,200 to £72,000 and £7770 to £9940 respectively. These ratios tell you that the plan is being successfully executed.

In this instance, I was able to use non-statutory information provided by management – number of stores open and total store operating lease rentals – alongside statutory information – sales, profit and numbers employed – to devise ratios that specifically enabled me to monitor the success of a stated management objective.

Hargreaves Lansdown

I have always thought that one of the strongest attractions of a business is scalability and Hargreaves Lansdown (HL) exhibits it in spades. HL is the leading provider of self-select, advisory and discretionary investment management products and services to UK private investors. It is a business where staff costs to sales have fallen from 38.2% in 2006 to 13.4% in 2015. Concurrently, sales and profit per employee have risen from £143,200 to £434,200 and £47,300 to £217,600 respectively. Human capital is becoming much more productive and profitable as the business grows.

The reason is that once the systems are put in place, maintained and periodically upgraded, more and more revenue can be generated from them. Like Halstead, there are occasional peaks of capex but, unlike Halstead, tangible fixed assets account for just 5% of net assets.

This lack of appetite for capital means HL is a prodigious generator of cash: its cash conversion ratio over the last ten years is 101%. Since it doesn't need this amount of cash to reinvest, it has been paying out in dividends 90% or more of its earnings since flotation in 2007. Yet, retained earnings still constitute a staggering 99% of capital and reserves. A very strong business indeed.

It is often true that a business light on physical assets is reliant on human capital to give it an edge. In the case of HL, this is a 'people' business where the skills of the staff are the bedrock of the investment case. The key then becomes how much revenue can be put through the existing systems set-up before an incremental addition is required. By concentrating on the development of the per capita ratios and the proportion of HL's costs that are represented by its highly paid staff, it can be seen that the answer is very much indeed. This is the essence of what we mean by scalability.

Long-term ratio analysis

Study of financial ratios over a long period of time is one of the most powerful tools of analysis available. Statistics compiled over ten or 20 years very rarely lie unless there has been a major change in the shape of the business. Also, such a study readily identifies the issues being faced by a company. If you refer back to the analysis sections of the James Halstead story, you will see that there are some very detailed explanations of what has happened, and is still happening, inside the business. To get this requires that questions be put to management. Ratio analysis provides the questions.

* * *

We now move on from consideration of the quality of business to how it might be valued in Chapter Nine. We end with some thoughts on portfolio construction in Chapter Ten.

CHAPTER NINE.
Valuation Techniques

"If calculus were needed, I'd have to go back to delivering papers."

— WARREN BUFFETT

I T IS OFTEN SAID THAT THE VALUATION OF A COMPANY IS MORE art than science. If there is some truth in that, it is because valuation is more a matter of judgement, i.e. balancing the consideration of many factors, rather than the unthinking application of strict mathematical formulae.

The knowledge of how to value a capital asset properly is probably *the* most valuable weapon in an investor's armoury. Warren Buffett said that if he were teaching a course on investing, there would be one valuation study after another with the students trying to identify the key variables in each particular business and evaluating how predictable they were.

Buffett learned this from his mentor, Ben Graham, whose classes were all about valuing companies. He would present his students with figures about Companies A and B and ask them to perform an evaluation. Sometimes, at the end of the exercise, they would be told that A and B were actually the same company at different points in its history. He was attempting to educate the mind to think about which variables are relevant or perhaps dominant.

The art of valuation is to identify and understand these key variables and then work out how predictable they are. If they are not predictable, close the book and move on. But if you can identify the dominant variables, you can then move onto the science part. That involves formulating a financial model to reflect how the business operates and makes its money. Such models cannot be relied upon to provide an exact valuation though. There are no absolutes in valuation; you are looking for the range of values that you think the business might be worth.

In this chapter, I will run over some of the common valuation metrics, and also some of the more esoteric ones. Of course, all relate price (i.e. your stock market entry ticket) to a metric usually drawn from the profit and loss account, balance sheet or cash flow statement. Some of these, such as price to earnings and price to book value, have been around a long time. Others, including those I dub 'esoteric' haven't. Included in the latter category are measures like price-earnings growth factor and enterprise value to EBITDA.

The problem is that none of these measures capture the potential future value creation inherent in a business beyond a year or two. So I take a look at a couple of models, not measures, that purport to do just this – namely the compounding earnings model and, my chosen favourite, discounted cash flow.

Before going into more detail, there are a couple of other points I need to air in relation to financial investors versus strategic investors and enterprise value versus equity value.

Financial investor versus strategic investor

In company valuation, the perspective of the valuer is very important. A financial investor will view the company as a standalone entity, basing judgement on the risk-adjusted financial returns likely to be secured from an investment in the company. The return must compare favourably with opportunities elsewhere, e.g. property, bonds or other companies. One financial investor has no theoretical advantage over any other financial investor and, in receipt of the same information and under identical assumptions, ought to arrive at much the same valuation as any of the peer group.

In practice, however, different financial investors frequently arrive at widely differing valuations – perhaps as well since it takes two views to make a market.

These differences arise for two good reasons. Firstly, a conceptual difference of view as to what is the best guide to value: sales, profits, earnings, cash flow or assets. Secondly, differences in the assumptions made: some investors may simply be better informed than others, maybe even acting on illegal inside information.

Conversely, a strategic investor might be able to secure additional value over and above that available to the financial investor, even with only partial ownership of the company. These extra gains derive from synergies between what is already owned and the new acquisition. Examples include economies of scale or access to new products and markets.

In principle, therefore, a strategic investor will usually place a higher value on a company than a financial investor. This explains why takeovers almost always occur at prices well above those ruling in the stock market immediately prior to the initial offer. The nature and size of such gains will be investor-specific. In this chapter, we are concerned only with the financial investor.

Equity value and enterprise value

There is an important distinction to be made at the outset between equity value and enterprise value. Equity value is that relating to the ordinary shares only and therefore the company's market capitalisation is meant to be a snapshot of this at any given time. Enterprise value is that of the company as a whole. It is measured as equity value plus debt minus cash. In general, if the valuation relies upon a metric struck before financial income and expense has been accounted for, it is valuing the enterprise. If struck after, it is valuing the equity.

Accounting models of valuation

The first port of call in looking at valuation is to look at the accounting models of valuation.

The traditional accounting model of company valuation says that share prices are determined by capitalising an accounting metric at an appropriate multiple. The accounting model centres on the income statement and the balance sheet.

Price to earnings ratio

Without doubt, the price to earnings ratio (PER) is the most widely used multiple-based valuation ratio. The concept of valuing a company by taking a multiple of earnings makes intuitive sense. The justification is that in the long run, earnings theoretically translate into cash. It is easy to imagine someone being willing to pay several times the earnings now in one lump sum to secure the benefits from a stream of earnings stretching out into the future. That is exactly what you do when you purchase an annuity for retirement income.

The PER is defined as the current share price divided by the earnings per share (EPS). At the company level, this translates into the market capitalisation divided by earnings, i.e. profit after tax and any minority interests and preference dividends. It is usual to take prospective EPS or earnings for this calculation, rather than historic.

The PER can be thought of as the number of years it will take the company to earn back the amount of the initial downpayment – assuming that the company's earnings remain static. If they were in secular decline, an investor would not want to pay as much as if they were growing rapidly. Hence growth companies tend to sport higher PERs, making the PER closely related to the prospects of the business and the industry in which it operates.

Other economic factors that affect the PER are the outlook for inflation and interest rates. In a climate of lower interest rates, the discounted net present value (NPV) of future earnings is enhanced because the discount factor (being governed by the interest rate environment) is lower. Similarly, the lower the inflation rate, the higher the real value of the future earnings, because they are not being eroded by the diminishing purchasing power of money.

Table 9.1 shows how interest rates and inflation affect the NPV of identical earnings over a four-year period (in reality the forecasts would stretch into perpetuity). The table shows the damage that higher interest rates and inflation inflict on value. For the same nominal earnings stream, the cumulative NPV at a 6% discount rate with no inflation is 104.2p. Discounted at 10% with 6% inflation, this falls to 84.1p. What this means in practice is that an investor who would have been prepared to pay a PER of 20x under the first set of circumstances might only be prepared to concede around 16x under the second (84.1 ÷ 104.2 x 20 = 16.1).

	Year 0	Year 1	Year 2	Year 3	Sum of NPV, Years 0-3
Earnings forecasts (growth @ 25% p.a.)	20.0	25.0	31.3	39.1	
Discounted @ 6%, no inflation	20.0	23.6	27.8	32.8	104.2
Discounted @ 10%, no inflation	20.0	22.7	25.8	29.4	97.9
Discounted @ 6%, 3% inflation	19.4	22.2	25.5	29.1	96.2
Discounted @ 10%, 3% inflation	19.4	21.4	23.6	26.1	90.5
Discounted @ 6%, 6% inflation	18.9	21.0	23.3	26.0	89.2
Discounted @ 10%, 6% inflation	18.9	20.2	21.7	23.3	84.1

Table 9.1 – Effect of discount factor (interest) and inflation on net present value (figures in pence)

Earnings yield

The earnings yield is the reciprocal of the PER expressed as a percentage. Thus a PER of 12.5 translates into an earnings yield of 8%. It was only in the 1960s that the PER (an American concept) assumed superiority over the traditional earnings yield.

The earnings yield must not be confused with the dividend yield. The owners of a business have a claim on the earnings irrespective of how much is actually paid out in dividends. Earnings retained are available for reinvestment, so generating additional wealth for the owners in the future.

The earnings yield shows the initial rate of return you can expect from the earnings upon which you have a claim, expressed as a percentage of the price you have paid. If you adopt Warren Buffett's view that equities can be looked upon as a type of bond, then the earnings yield becomes the equivalent of the bond's coupon. The exception is that the yield is usually fixed in the case of a bond but is variable – and hopefully expanding – in the case of equities. The earnings yield enables you to make a direct comparison with non-equity types of investment such as government securities (gilts), corporate bonds or deposit accounts.

Before the Second World War, equities had earnings yields much higher than those available on gilts because conventional wisdom was that this compensated equity investors for the additional risk that they bore. The difference was known as the *yield gap*. Then came the concept of growth. Valuable businesses increase their earnings, so the earnings yield expands. The cult of equity was born and earnings yields fell below those of gilts, creating a *reverse yield gap*. That is still broadly true today, though the ultra-low interest rate environment in the wake of the Great Recession of 2008/9 has distorted it.

PEG factor

One problem with the PER, and by implication the earnings yield, is that it is a one-dimensional number, not obviously related to any other accepted measure of value. It says nothing about the likely future growth rate of earnings, or whether they are accelerating or decelerating. Nor does it say whether one company with an identical rate of earnings growth to another is able to achieve that growth with the same level of investment. Lastly, it is indifferent to the opportunity cost of capital, i.e. what return is available from an alternative investment with the same risk-reward profile.

A refinement is the price-earnings growth factor, or PEG for short. This was another American concept that was transported across the Atlantic and championed by Jim Slater in his *Zulu Principle* books. It relates the familiar PER to the projected growth rate of earnings over the same period by dividing the former by the latter. Thus a company selling on a PER of 10 with a growth rate of 15% has a PEG of 10 ÷ 15 = 0.67. It is an attempt to get away from the one-dimensional character of the PER by relating the price you pay for a given amount of earnings to what you can expect by way of future growth of those earnings.

You certainly want the PEG to be less than 1 and ideally less than 0.75. However, there is a good mathematical reason why the relationship between the PER and the earnings growth is not linear. The numerator, the PER, is linear but the denominator, EPS growth, introduces a geometric progression into the ratio as compounding starts to work. This non-linearity is a weakness of the PEG and it is laid bare in Table 9.2.

Sanford: Share price 100p; forecast EPS 10p; EPS growth rate 10%; PER = 10x; PEG = 1.0

Year	1	2	3	4	5	6	7	8	9
EPS (p)	10.0	11.0	12.1	13.3	14.6	16.2	17.7	19.5	21.4
Cumulative EPS (p)	10.0	21.0	33.1	46.4	61.0	77.2	94.9	114.4	135.8

Time taken to recover initial share price in earnings: 7 years, 96 days

DeLand: Share price 200p; forecast EPS 10p; EPS growth rate 20%; PER = 20x; PEG = 1.0

Year	1	2	3	4	5	6	7	8	9
EPS (p)	10.0	12.0	14.4	17.3	20.7	24.9	29.9	35.8	43.0
Cumulative EPS (p)	10.0	22.0	36.4	53.7	74.4	99.3	129.2	165.0	208.0

Time taken to recover initial share price in earnings: 8 years, 297 days

Table 9.2 – The non-linear relationship between PER and PEG

In effect, if the PER is really a form of annuity, the PEG overvalues companies where the PER is high and vice versa. See how the high PER DeLand takes longer to earn back its original purchase price than the low PER Sanford: 8.81 years versus 7.26. This means that PEGs lose more of their utility the higher the PER and it is a powerful argument for only using them in combination with a PER cut-off. Jim Slater, for example, found that PEGs work best with the PER in the range of 12-20 and EPS growth rates of 15-25%.

Though better than the PER alone, the PEG still has a habit of making smaller dynamic growth companies look pretty fully valued at the outset. Also, by only looking at the PEG one year out, you are capturing but a small portion of the earning power of companies, which, after all, are set up to trade indefinitely.

Enterprise value to operating profit ratios

This is a similar concept to the PER except that the profit measure is struck before interest and tax. Therefore the correct comparator is enterprise value. It is usual to add back to operating profit any amortisation charge relating to goodwill or acquired intangible assets. For that reason, the ratio is sometimes lazily termed EV/ EBITA, despite the fact that earnings are technically struck post-tax.

Another variant that has found favour among investment bankers is EV/EBITDA. My views on EBITDA have been strongly expressed already. I regard it as a worthless metric because it is struck before depreciation. Depreciation, unlike amortisation (except of software), is a real cost to a business, being a provision to replace worn out productive assets.

Enterprise value to sales ratio

The enterprise value to sales ratio (EVSR) relates EV to annual turnover but is nearly always incorrectly termed the price to sales ratio. It is traditionally used in 'black hole' valuations where there are no profits and where cash flow can be severely compromised.

The importance of taking turnover is to provide a measure of the company's potential value. For a cyclical, this is important if and when it recovers, and the EVSR will normally be low. For a start-up company or one in a development phase, it is the future potential as the company matures and begins to generate earnings and cash. Here the EVSR might be high.

Companies already in a phase of strong growth will possess a higher EVSR than average. This is not just because the market is anticipating a faster rate of top-line growth, but also because such companies usually enjoy higher operating margins, i.e. they make more profit out of every £1 of revenue. The EVSR tends to decline as the company gets bigger, reflecting the fact that it is easier to grow rapidly from a low base. If you pay too high a multiple for those sales and the turnover growth fails to materialise, or the company loses an important contract, the impact on the bottom line can be calamitous.

Simplistically, once a given level of sales covers the fixed or establishment costs, the company is past its break-even point and incremental gross profit falls through to the bottom line. Conversely, take a big chunk out of sales and the effect on the bottom line is disproportionate in the other direction; particularly where they are high-margin sales. This is known as operational gearing and should not be confused with financial gearing, which is net debt as a percentage of equity shareholders' funds.

In passing, I must point out that a combination of high operational gearing and high financial gearing is a lethal cocktail.

Price to cash flow

Price to cash flow (PCF) is not dissimilar to the PER. PCF is the company's market capitalisation divided by its cash flow. The problem is the lack of a generally accepted definition of cash flow. It should be the cash generated from operations before any discretionary expenditure. To me, discretionary expenditure means acquisitions or obvious expansionary capex, such as building a new factory, as opposed to capex to maintain existing facilities. In other words, free cash flow. To others, it can mean as little as accounting earnings after adding back depreciation and amortisation. As with the PER, PCF has a reciprocal known as the cash flow yield. Personally, I believe there are much better means of attempting to value using cash flow, which we will come to later.

Price to book value

Price to book value (PBV) is an attempt to relate the share price to the net asset value. Book value is not meant to be the value of the company; it is merely the carrying value of the net assets recorded in the balance sheet. As such, it is subject to all the accounting distortions and equity equivalents I mentioned when discussing economic profit. In particular, it includes intangible assets alongside tangibles, so a better measure to take might be price to tangible asset value, excluding items such as goodwill.

* * *

This completes the review of ratios that relate price to a metric drawn directly from company accounts. Whilst useful, all of what we have considered have their limitations. We will now move from metrics to models in our quest to find a robust valuation methodology.

Compounding earnings model

I sometimes use the compounding earnings model to try to get a feel for the intrinsic value of a company and the return an investment might generate over a period of time. In contrast to multiple-based valuations, this assessment attempts to value a share independently of its current market price. We are trying to determine what a share is worth, i.e. the price at which it should sell if properly priced in a normal market.

The manner in which to go about this is to estimate what an investor today is likely to have in value at the end of a given holding period (typically five years), which is added to the dividends received along the way to compute the total return.

Step one is to value the equity at the end of five years by capitalising an estimate of the following year's earnings at that time. The starting point is the value of shareholders' funds today, to which is added back any goodwill or acquired intangible assets that have been previously written-off to reserves or amortised. This is gross equity, as mentioned before.

Next, calculate the current return being achieved on this. The return is simply the earnings of the business after all taxes, interest, minority interests and preference dividends have been paid for the most recent financial period. The average of the opening and closing gross equity is what this return has been achieved on.

Before this level can be used to project forwards, you have to be satisfied that the business can continue to earn this return on all future reinvested earnings. To be sustainable, the franchise must be capable of further expansion to achieve rates of return comparable to those achieved in the past. Obviously if returns are already faltering (as evidenced by a persistent lower marginal return) this is unlikely. Also, the franchise must not be close to saturation maturity or currently benefiting from exceptional pricing opportunities that might close.

Assuming confidence of such sustainability, future earnings are projected by applying the present return on equity to the opening shareholder equity, as increased by retained earnings, year after year to the end of the projection period. Retained earnings, which increase the equity, are struck after what is actually paid out in dividends. The retention/pay-out ratio that I use is the average for the last five financial years excluding special dividends. To illustrate these concepts, Table 9.3 applies them to the example of A.G. Barr plc.

Year to January	2016E	2017E	2018E	2019E	2020E	2021E
Return on gross equity (%)	21.2	21.2	21.2	21.2	21.2	21.2
Retention ratio (%)	58.8	58.8	58.8	58.8	58.8	58.8
Opening gross equity	160.5	180.5	203.0	228.3	256.8	288.8
Earnings for the year	34.0	38.3	43.0	48.4	54.4	61.2
Dividends paid out	-14.0	-15.8	-17.7	-19.9	-22.4	-25.2
Earnings retained	20.0	22.5	25.3	28.5	32.0	36.0
Closing gross equity	180.5	203.0	228.3	256.8	288.8	324.8
Value of equity (PER 15)	574.5	645.0	726.0	816.0	918.0	
Total dividends received	14.0	29.8	47.5	76.0	98.4	
Projected market capitalisation					1,016.4	
Present market capitalisation					622.4	
Compound rate of return (%)					10.3	

Table 9.3 – A.G. Barr plc, compounding earnings model valuation (£m unless stated)

Barr is a producer and distributor of carbonated and still soft drinks and bottled water. Its best known brand is IRN-BRU (Scotland's favourite soft drink). It is a brand builder with a stable operating model and steadily improving results going back more than ten years. Recently, it has been up against tough comparatives, with 2014 having benefited from the Glasgow Commonwealth Games at that time. Also it has been moving its carton and multi packing facilities from Tredegar to Milton Keynes, entailing a bulge in capex and double running costs for a while.

Over the last five years, this business has generated a return on gross equity of between 20.6% and 21.7%, the average return being 21.2%. Moreover, its marginal returns, calculated over successive three-year periods, have been between 18.8% and 24.5%, giving some confidence of sustainability. Its retention ratio has varied between 57% and 59.8%, with the average being 58.8%.

At the end of year five, we have an earnings expectation for the following year (2021) of £61.2m. Now comes the familiar problem: how to capitalise this at an appropriate multiple.

In the classic compounding earnings model, we would use the reciprocal of the current yield on the benchmark 10-year government bond. That is because the earnings could be replaced at present by the interest that comes from buying a multiple of their value in gilts. But in an ultra-low interest rate environment, this can imply a capitalisation multiple of over 50x!

An alternative might be to use the current prospective PER multiple. In the case of A.G. Barr, this is 18.5x based on consensus earnings estimates for 2016. This projects £1,132.2m for the value of equity.

Another alternative, which I favour, is to take the long-run average PER of the UK stock market, which is about 15x. This would reduce the projected value of equity to £918m. Now all that is needed is to total up the dividends paid out in the five years (£98.4m) and add this to the value of the equity (£918m). This is the total return expected on the investment – in this case £1,016.4m. Comparing this to the current price, the compounding rate of return is 10.3% per annum going forwards.

To be attractive, the rate of return must compensate an investor for inflation and personal taxation on both capital gains and income, and leave sufficient real return to make it worthwhile taking the risk of investing in equities. Personally, I think a 15% compounding rate is where investments start to look really attractive. Ten percent, though, is fine. Five percent and you are in danger of obtaining no real return.

Effectively, the compounding model relies upon five input factors:

1. Present market capitalisation

2. Capitalisation rate (PER)

3. Return on equity

4. Starting shareholder equity

5. Pay-out ratio

There is no question about 1 and 4 and little argument about what to use for 3 and 5. But as we have seen, 2 is more subjective and has the scope to introduce errors. Another weakness of the model is that present returns on equity (3) may not prove to be sustainable. It goes without saying that if the company stumbles financially, the model fails. The strength of the model is that it incorporates return on equity as a central pillar.

The compounding earnings model certainly has something to offer. Like multiple-based ratios, though, it is based on the accounting model of valuation. Let's now turn to an alternative, discounted cash flow, which is based upon the economic model of valuation.

The economic model of valuation

Simple formulae like those used in the accounting model have clear attractions for investors but they fall short on a number of criteria:

1. What other company or investment class should you make the comparison with to determine the appropriate multiple to get to implied value?

2. Multiples are not static. They change in light of all kinds of movements in the dynamics of the underlying business and general economic conditions.

3. Profit, earnings and asset measurement, even revenue recognition, are subjective in their calculation. For example, it matters if these metrics can be boosted by capitalising a cash outlay in the balance sheet rather than expensing it through the income statement.

4. Earnings do not always reflect the cash flows of the business.

5. Earnings do not reflect the rate of return a company earns on its invested capital.

By contrast, the economic model of company valuation focuses on the sources and uses of cash. So it doesn't matter where the cash outlays get recorded. Business Perspective Investors care only about how much cash seems likely to be generated over the lifetime of the business and the risk that it won't materialise. Growth is important in that a good business will be able to expand its cash earnings (effectively its coupon) at a higher rate than the discount rate used to bring those future cash earnings back to present value.

The discounted cash flow model

Discounted cash flow (DCF) is the most thorough valuation technique. It allows analysis of every element of cash flow in a business. It then relates the company's value to future cash flows by discounting them back to NPV. Owing to its thoroughness, DCF is the technique most commonly used by companies to estimate value when making an acquisition.

Most companies are not set up to operate for a period of one or two years and then disappear from the face of the earth. They continue in perpetuity. So what sense does it make to try and value a company on the basis of one or two years' earnings? This is the problem with most multiple-based valuation methods, such as the PER and the PEG. There is value beyond the two years and, in any case, the earnings are only useful as a valuation shortcut if they translate into cash, which is often not the case.

Imagine that you only plan to hold the shares for five years. Along the way you will see five years' worth of cash flows, but at the end you will have an asset of capital value. If you sell at this point, you are effectively liquidating and the worth of the asset to whoever buys it from you is the break-up value or the future stream of flows that the buyer has identified. In your case, the price at which you can sell the asset is called *terminal* or *residual value*.

Discounted cash flow valuation relies upon an assessment of all future revenues generated and costs incurred by the company. Hence, it cannot be undertaken lightly because it requires so much detailed information on the enterprise as input factors. The downside is the sensitivity to the assumptions made in forecasting the cash flows and, crucially, to the discount rate applied in arriving at net present value.

In making projections, it is usual to have the specific forecast period during which explicit assumptions about the development of revenues, margins and all costs are made. Beyond that certain period, there is a 'steady state' default assumption put into place, which assumes that long-run growth will approximate to the inflation-adjusted rate of growth of the economy in which the business operates.

In the classic model, the discount rate applied is the company's weighted average cost of capital (WACC). WACC is the proportion of debt in the enterprise value of the company multiplied by the company's current borrowing rate, plus the proportion of equity multiplied by the expected return on the company's equity.

The expected return on equity is governed by the capital asset pricing model (CAP-M), which, in turn, is the child of the efficient markets hypothesis (EMH). It is market determined and usually based on a gilt yield of comparable maturity to the specific forecast period. A premium is then attached to this risk-free rate to reflect the additional risk profile of the company being valued. This premium consists of a market risk premium multiplied by the volatility of the company's share price in relation to the market (called the stock's beta). I work on the basis that real risk is business based, i.e. how risky is the company and its markets, and this has nothing to do with share price volatility. For this and other reasons, I believe the whole edifice of EMH and CAP-M is built on sand.

So as with economic profit, I adopt a simpleton's approach by turning the whole thing on its head. I think that a rational expectation for an equity investor is to achieve a compounding total return of 10% per annum. This then becomes the company's cost of equity and it is this 10% that I use to discount future cash flows. I ignore the proportion of debt in the company's capital structure (debt is always cheaper than equity). Admittedly, using 10% is a high hurdle, but better to err on the side of conservatism when investing.

In addition to receiving specific future free cash flows, the investor owns the terminal value. This can also be discounted back to NPV at the outset, in one of three ways:

1. **Growth-based approach**. Assume steady state growth of the cash flows in perpetuity and work out their discounted value using Gordon's growth model. This states that the present value (P) of a stream of future cash flows is as follows – where C is the next year's cash flow, d is the discount rate and g is the expected growth rate in perpetuity for the cash flows:

   $$P = C \div (d - g)$$

2. **Market-based approach**. Capitalise the final year's discounted cash flow on the multiple prevailing for a sample of comparable companies.

3. **Asset-based approach**. Discount book value or shareholders' funds at the end of the forecast period back to present value.

The most common method, and the one that I invariably use, is the growth-based residual value calculation. I normally prepare specific forecasts going out three years. Then I look at the company's return on equity and its retention ratio. The earnings growth rate is then the product of the ROE and the retention ratio. I will use this growth rate for years 4-5 of the projection period, halve it for years 6-10 and then assume steady state growth at rates comparable to growth in long-run Western world GDP, i.e. 2.5% per annum.

Table 9.4 shows a worked example of how I might perform a quick DCF, in this case again using A.G. Barr plc. The free cash flow growth rate of 11.8% used after the explicit forecast comes from the latest ROE of 20.6% multiplied by the latest 57% retention ratio. The estimated fair value per share (478p) is, at the time of writing, about 9% below the share price. The implication is that your target 10%

compounding annual total return on your investment is going to depend upon dividends paid out. This means that you are certainly not getting £1 of capital value at a discount based on these estimates and the current share price.

A. Explicit forecast period (A=Actual, F=Forecast)

Year to January	2014A	2015A	2016F	2017F	2018F
Turnover	254.1	260.9	261.0	272.0	284.0
Profit before interest & tax	34.7	38.8	41.8	44.3	46.9
Depreciation & Amortisation	6.7	7.0	8.0	9.0	10.0
Other trading items*	0.3	0.9	0.3	0.6	0.6
Gross cash flow	41.7	46.7	50.1	53.9	57.5
Interest received (paid)	-0.4	-0.2	-0.8	-0.3	0.1
Taxes paid	-7.7	-7.0	-8.6	-9.0	-9.4
Net cash flow	33.6	39.5	40.7	44.6	48.2
Working capital	7.8	5.1	0.0	-0.9	-2.2
Capital expenditure	-13.3	-18.0	-24.0	-15.0	-12.0
Free cash flow	28.1	26.6	16.7	28.7	34.0
Discount rate (%)**	-	-	1.6	10.0	10.0
NPV of free cash flow	-	-	16.4	25.7	27.7

B. Non-explicit Forecast Period

Year to January (£m unless stated)	2019	2020	2021	2022	2023	2024	2025	2026
Growth in free cash on prior year (%)	11.8	11.8	5.9	5.9	5.9	5.9	5.9	2.5
Free cash flow	38.1	42.5	45.1	47.7	50.5	53.5	56.7	58.1
Discount rate (%)	10	10	10	10	10	10	10	10
NPV of free cash flow	28.1	28.6	27.5	26.5	25.5	24.6	23.7	22.0

C. DCF Valuation

	Actual	NPV
NPV of free cash flow 2016-18	79.4	69.8
NPV of free cash flow 2019-25	334.1	184.5
NPV of free cash flow after 2025***	774.5	323.3
		577.6
Add cash / deduct debt		-19.8
Enterprise value		557.8
Fully diluted shares in issue (m)		116.8
Fair value per share (p)		478

Table 9.4 – Simple DCF valuation, A.G. Barr plc (£m unless stated)

Notes to Table 9.4:

* Impairment, loss (gain) on fixed asset sales, share-based payments & pension top-up payments

** DCF prepared two months from end of financial year, hence lower discount rate for 2016

*** Gordon's growth model: NPV = 2026 FCF £59.1m ÷ (discount rate – growth rate) 7.5%

If this all sounds rather complicated, it's because it is. But fortunately there is a short cut that you can employ. Another beauty of using a 10% discount factor is this:

A.G. Barr generated £26.6m of free cash flow in 2015. Valued as an annuity and discounted back at 10% places an NPV of £266m on the stream of cash (£26.6m ÷ 0.1). You can compare this with the market capitalisation – £613m at the time of writing. This implies that 43% (266 ÷ 613) of the present market value is represented by the existing business with 57% representing the growth yet to be delivered by management's forward plan. In an ideal situation you want 100% of the present market capitalisation to be represented by the existing business meaning that you are getting the prospect of the forward plan thrown in for free.

By way of conclusion to this chapter, the tables below provide a summary of the pros and cons of the two most common valuation methods. It goes without saying that my preference is for economic models and a focus on cash, not profits. However, it is always instructive to use a number of methods and compare the outcomes.

Pros and cons of PER

Advantages of PER	Disadvantages of PER
Simple and relatively quick to apply	Cannot deal with erratic trading
Availability of historic data for benchmarking	Does not assume business will continue in perpetuity
Method most commonly used by the press and financial analysts	Assumes profit is always a satisfactory proxy for cash

Pros and cons of DCF

Advantages of DCF	Disadvantages of DCF
Captures information regarding future income growth trends	Subjectivity: assumptions made and choice of discount rate
Based on cash rather than profit	Methods of dealing with residual value
Allows sensitivity analysis to be run on key valuation parameters	Lack of market benchmarks against which to judge valuation

CHAPTER TEN.
Portfolio Management

"There are a relatively small number of truly outstanding companies. Their shares frequently can't be bought at attractive prices. Therefore, when favourable prices exist, full advantage should be taken of the situation."

— PHILIP FISHER

GREAT INVESTMENT OPPORTUNITIES OFTEN ARISE WHEN excellent companies are affected by unusual circumstances that cause their share prices to be wrongly appraised. Having identified an outstanding company, you must be sure that its shares can be bought for substantially less than their true economic worth.

In this chapter, I will discuss when is the right time to buy and sell an equity holding, what is the nature of the risk you are taking on board, how you should concentrate your portfolio in investments that you have great conviction in, and how important dividends are likely to be to your total return.

Margin of safety

As well as concerning itself with evaluating the quality of a business, Business Perspective Investment is as much the craft of buying a £1 coin for much less than £1. To practice it successfully requires two things only. Firstly, you must have the knowledge to enable you to make a rough estimate about the intrinsic value of an underlying business. That's what Chapter Nine was all about. Secondly, you must have the intellectual rigour to ensure that you only buy into that business at substantially less than you believe it to be worth.

Successful investment demands that there be a material difference between the price you pay and the value you get. This is your margin of safety and it is only the closing of that price-value gap that gives you your super-normal investment profit. There can be no super-normal profit potential if a company's share price is always equal to its intrinsic value. And the one factor, more than any other, that determines the return from a financial asset is the price you pay for it in the first instance.

Fortunately, markets are neither efficient nor rational all the time. Market price and business value may be apart for weeks, months or even years. You cannot predict the time it will take for the gap to close, but you know that it will eventually. The only slight fly in the ointment is Keynes' admonition that the market can stay irrational for longer than you can stay solvent! Investment analysis always involves considering both value and price; the way to give yourself the best chance of success is to get more in value than you pay in price.

All else being equal, you don't need as large a discount to intrinsic value when buying a high returns company as you do for one with a ho-hum return on capital. You'll get an attractive cash earnings yield at the outset plus future growth in the value of the business.

Risk and diversification

Modern Portfolio Theory (MPT) postulates that the more holdings there are in a fund, the more risk is reduced. That is because it equates risk with share price volatility, not the underlying economics of the business. Of course, if you need to liquidate, there is a real risk that prices might be against you on any given day. But you shouldn't be investing in equities if your time horizon is that short and you can't afford to ride the dips.

As you know, I don't buy into MPT. I favour concentrating investments in relatively few companies that I think I know a lot about. I typically have ownership of around

25-35 holdings in appropriate companies. Conventional portfolio diversification is little more than a hedge against having the courage of your convictions.

I view real risk as being that of investing in the wrong businesses. And by loading more and more companies into your portfolio, you are almost certainly adding businesses at the margin that you know relatively less about than your earlier high conviction investments. That heightens the risk of backing a dud. So I believe that over-diversification actually increases business risk.

Whilst I accept that concentration might increase share price volatility, I don't worry about this because I prefer a bumpy 15% average annual return to a smooth 10%.

Focus investing

The opportunity for practitioners of focused investing was neatly summarised by Warren Buffett speaking to the New York Society of Security Analysts:

> "A lot of great fortunes in this world have been made by owning a single wonderful business. If you understand the business, you don't need to own very many of them."

The problem with conventional portfolio diversification is that it increases the chances of making investments in too many companies that too little is known about. So I restrict myself to those businesses that firstly I understand and that secondly I know most about. This is what I mean by limiting myself to my 'circle of competence'. Too many investors' circles of competence seem to be a mile wide and an inch deep. Mine is quite the opposite. I always aim to invest in a spread of superior businesses that I know well, which I believe reduces economic risk.

There seems to be a widespread antipathy to running concentrated (i.e. lesser diversified) portfolios. Yet it is ironic that index tracker funds are usually regarded as being lower risk. According to FTSE International Limited in its fact sheet dated 31 December 2015, the FTSE All-Share Index had a market capitalisation of £2.03 trillion. Of this, the top ten constituents accounted for £617 billion, or 30.3% of the total. This, in fact, makes any trackers of that index – and indeed similar indices which share these characteristics of a small number of large companies dominating them – highly concentrated, with an enormous tail.

My advice would be to select a few companies that are likely to produce above-average returns over the long run and then concentrate the majority of your investments in their shares. Next, make sure you have the mental strength to hold steady during any short-term market ructions. This is the antithesis of what most people think that portfolio management is, or should be, about. It is as Warren Buffett is to Gordon Gekko.

What could be more sensible than buying a meaningful interest in a simple business selling at an undemanding price-to-value ratio rather than small amounts of complex businesses with not much margin of safety? Then you stick with the simple business and let its operational performance improve over time. Focus investors, like poker players, bet big when they believe the odds are in their favour.

When to sell

Once committed to an investment, I let the operating performance of the company tell me how successful the investment has been, not the share price. This is because I am a long-term partner who believes that the principal risk for investors is business-based, not stock market price-based.

There is another advantage of long-term holding in the form of keeping portfolio turnover down. Repeated buying and selling incurs transaction costs on exit and re-entry, such as broking fees, levies and stamp duty. These frictional costs detract from returns over time.

Having said that, I might sell a portfolio investment for one of the following reasons:

1. **Mistake made**. The reality is a lot less favourable than you had originally envisaged. Every decisive person makes mistakes: so admit them, learn from them and resolve not to repeat them. Mentally rub your nose in it, as Charlie Munger would say. Investor ego is often assuaged when, having made a mistake, the shares can be offloaded at a small profit. Unwillingness to take a loss, however small, often causes investors to hang on until they can come out even, with even worse results. You rarely make back money in the same thing you lost money in to start with. Treat a losing investment as a losing investment and cut the loss.

2. **Permanent deterioration**. This could apply to the franchise, its growth prospects or its management. Disruptive technologies are a potent threat, as investors in Eastman Kodak could testify. Faced with technological obsolescence, Kodak took some of its patent proceeds and cash flow and invested outside its core competence in another declining business – printers. It ended up being decimated by its own invention of digital photography! Sometimes it may be

that after a spectacular burst of growth, a company has simply exhausted the potential of its markets. It moves to being a sluggard or stalwart, suffering PER compression in the process. Probably the most common cause though is a change and deterioration of management. Either the new lot try to diversify or don't have the ability, drive and ingenuity to keep the company on the straight and narrow.

3. **Switching**. Here an alternative superior investment has been found but you have not got spare cash to buy it. Switching is potentially dangerous because you risk trading old gold for gilded plastic. Holding an investment for some time usually provides a good insight into the business's characteristics – warts and all – that might be lacking in the new one.

4. **Over-inflated asset prices**. Every now and again, in the midst of an asset bubble, market prices become detached from economic reality. The dot-com boom and bust is a prime example of this and the bond market at the time of writing in late 2015 may be the same. It can pay to take some money off the table. A more specific situation might be that an investee company has become substantially over-valued on a basis that might prove temporary. It has risen to heights that look ridiculous in relation to its history and peer group. Sage in the raging dot-com boom was an example of that, as we saw in Chapter Five.

5. **Nightmare on Throgmorton Street**. This is when a black swan economic event compounds an already deteriorating economic climate. A good example would be in October 1973 when oil prices quadrupled in the wake of the Yom Kippur War. The business climate had already been worsening prior to this with high inflation, higher interest rates and company failures. A double whammy like this usually fells **every** tree in the forest. Unfortunately, it is difficult to anticipate such events with foresight.

The worst reason of all to sell is solely to crystallise a profit. One of the best maxims is to run your profits and cut your losses. Unfortunately, this runs contrary to how most people are wired.

The importance of dividends

I prefer that companies reinvest their earnings wherever it is possible to do so at attractive high rates of return. And provided that by so doing, they create at least £1 of market value for each £1 of retained earnings, they are doing the right thing. Never forget that money paid out attracts the interest of the taxman, whereas when left in the company, it compounds up safe from his reach.

Reinvestment opportunities are where American companies with a large domestic market have such an advantage over British companies. There is so much more to go at before having to take the additional risk of expanding outside the home market. For example, Berkshire Hathaway has never paid a dividend; it always reinvests the cash back into existing businesses or makes acquisitions, and nearly always in the US.

Notwithstanding, dividend income does form an integral part of the total return of an investment; the other component being capital growth. Dividends are important for more than income generation, though. They provide a useful check during the process of assessing a company as an investment prospect that management is being rational about allocating capital.

It simply isn't possible to pay dividends year-in, year-out, without the company generating sufficient free cash to cover its reinvestment requirements and still having some cash left over at the end to reward its shareholders. The adoption of a progressive dividend policy, sometimes accompanied by periodic returns of surplus capital (via share buy-backs or special dividends) is an excellent sign that management has the owner's eye. Paying dividends, rather than hoarding cash more in hope than expectation, is a very good management trait.

Studies show that dividends form a consistently high proportion of the total return available from equities. During the 'lost decade' for equity investment from the start of 2000 to the end of 2009, the FTSE All-Share Index fell by over 15% from 3242 to 2751 but its counterpart, the Total Return Index, which is based on dividends reinvested, rose by almost 18% from 3051 to 3591.

Also, over the long-term, dividend-paying shares appear to perform better than their non-paying counterparts and deliver stronger relative returns in difficult economic times. Ben Graham and David Dodd first pointed out the investment paradox inherent in this. The more the shareholder subtracts in dividends from the capital and surplus fund, the larger value he seems to place upon what is left.

* * *

So there we have it. Only buy when you appear to be receiving more in value than you are being asked to pay in price. Concentrate your investments in companies you know well. Buy and hold for the long-term, letting the success of the investment be judged by how the company performs, not by its share price. Only sell when something looks to have gone wrong; never solely to crystallise a profit. And lastly, prefer highly profitable reinvestment to dividends, but dividends to the hoarding of cash for no apparent good reason.

CONCLUSION

I believe that there are ten essential differences between a good and a bad business. These are summarised in the table below.

Good business	Bad business
1. Simple	1. Complicated
2. Scalable and growing	2. Stagnant or declining
3. Good profitability	3. Poor profitability
4. Generates free cash	4. Absorbs cash
5. Predictable	5. Unpredictable
6. Good track record	6. Poor track record
7. Light on physical assets	7. Heavy on physical assets
8. Price maker	8. Price taker
9. Proprietary product	9. Commodity product
10. Focused management	10. Unfocused management

By thorough analysis of the company's competitive standing, its growth record, profitability of both sales and capital, and its ability to turn earnings into free cash, you will have 90% of what is needed to determine the shape of a business. The missing 10% is the more subjective judgement of management, particularly when much of the historic data was compiled under a previous team.

Once having determined the attraction of a company by the quality of its business, only then turn to valuation. I repeat my investment credo:

> An excellent business bought at an excellent price invariably makes an excellent investment over time.

You must only swing when there is an appreciable margin of safety between what you think you are receiving in economic worth against what you are being asked to pay in price. When there is, hit the ball hard and commit large amounts of capital to the investment.

Having made the investment, allow time and compounding to work their magic. Resist the temptation to sell a holding unless there is a very good specific reason. Avoid the temptation to sell solely to crystallise a profit. Run your profits and cut your losses. By so doing you will be well on the road to investment enlightenment and success.

INDEX

THANKS
FOR READING!

Our readers mean everything to us at Harriman House. As a special thank you for buying this book, let us help you save as much as possible on your next read:

1

If you've never ordered from us before, get £5 off your first order of £15 or more at **harriman-house.com** with this code: `iitb51`

Already a customer? Get £5 off an order of £25 or more with this code: `iitb25`

2

Get 7 days' FREE access to hundreds of our eBooks at **volow.co** – simply head to the website and sign up.

Thanks again!
from the team at

Harriman House

CPSIA information can be obtained
at www.ICGtesting.com
Printed in the USA
BVOW10*0926030816

457652BV00045B/195/P

9 780857 194848

3/18/18